# A PAGAN RITUAL PRAYER BOOK

# A PAGAN RITUAL PRAYER BOOK

Ceisiwr Serith

WEISERBOOKS
San Francisco, CA / Newburyport, MA

First published in 2011 by
Red Wheel/Weiser, LLC
With offices at:
500 Third Street, Suite 230
San Francisco, CA 94107
*www.redwheelweiser.com*

ISBN: 978-1-57863-484-2

Library of Congress Cataloging-in-Publication Data is available
on request.

Cover design by Jim Warner.
Interior design by Jane Hagaman.
Typeset in Giovanni and Stone Sans.

Printed in the United States of America
IBI

10   9   8   7   6   5   4   3

The paper used in this publication meets the minimum
requirements of the American National Standard for Information
Sciences—Permanence of Paper for Printed Library Materials
Z39.48-1992 (R1997).

*For my father,*
*who taught me to root for the referees.*

# ACKNOWLEDGMENTS

Many people helped in the writing of this book. Those who have willingly suffered through various rituals I've written while I honed my skills have gone above and beyond. Of these, I especially thank the members of my proto-grove, Nemos Ognios. The critiques of my work on the Ár nDraíocht Féin Liturgists Guild email list have helped me improve my style. It was Neal Levin who, by suggesting the book's structure, gave me the idea of writing from the point of view of a ritual.

I gladly thank my wife Debbie and my daughter Elizabeth for encouraging me and for providing me with an environment in which I could allow my thoughts to turn to religious matters. My time with two women who are so good with words has increased my own skill and, from the most personal point of view, most of what I know about the concerns of real people has come from them. Most especially, my wife has worked hard through the years, allowing me to take the time to discover that I could write. I couldn't have done it without her.

I've dedicated this book to my father. I owe him not just for the ethical training he gave through his dedication to fairness in sports, but for the encouragement this athletic man gave to a child who was so obviously intended for the more intellectual world. Much of who I am was formed by him. Thank you, Dad.

# Contents

# INTRODUCTION

"But Pagans don't pray!" Of course they do—some of our earliest records of Paganism are prayers. Look at the Homeric hymns, the *Rig Veda*, the Hittite cuneiform tablets. Look at the earliest ethnographic accounts of American Indians, Polynesians, African tribesmen. Prayers are everywhere in the Pagan literature.

In response to this misconception, I wrote *A Book of Pagan Prayer*, in which I gave several hundred examples of modern prayers and presented a theory of prayer to help people write their own. The success of that book has proven something: Pagans, even modern ones, do indeed pray.

Even after the publication of *A Book of Pagan Prayer*, I continued to write prayers—it's what I do. That led to this book.

*A Pagan Ritual Prayer Book* is in some ways a sequel, with even more prayers than my previous book. I've arranged it differently, however, so it can serve a slightly different purpose, to be of greater use in ritual. Pagans do pray for particular reasons, of course—for healing, prosperity, protection. *A Book of Pagan Prayer* dealt mainly with that kind of prayer. These have their place in this book as well.

There are, however, other kinds of prayers, those that form parts of rituals: starting them, accomplishing their aims, and bringing them to an end. These are prayers to encounter the sacred, to praise it, or often simply to acknowledge it. These are the prayers I concentrate on in this book.

Part I provides a discussion of prayer theory and gives an overview of the relationship between prayer and ritual. Part II follows the structure of a ritual, from calling people together to saying good-bye to both deities and people. Part III centers on petitionary prayers.

Before giving the prayers themselves, I've provided a discussion of prayer theory. This is not as extensive as in *A Book of Pagan Prayer*. My goal was to give enough information to allow this book to be useful on its own and to help people construct their own prayers, but without repeating too much from the previous book. I also wanted to present new material, things that I've learned since writing *A Book of Pagan Prayer* or that I didn't have the space to put in that book.

In one sense, then, this book stands alone, while in another it is a continuation and expansion of my previous work. I've tried to present the most important points in different ways, so even those who have seen them before can gain something from them. Because of the emphasis on ritual, I've added a chapter on ritual theory. I've only been able to touch on the most basic features of this broad topic, concentrating on those connected with prayer. For those interested in a deeper study I'm working on a book about ritual, where I will cover the subject in more detail.

In writing this book, I've tried to consider feedback from readers of *A Book of Pagan Prayer*. For instance, one reviewer suggested that a book written by a single author would tend to be limited to deities that had a particular appeal to that person. I'd actually made an effort to avoid that, but fair enough. I've made even more effort in this book to include a large number of deities from as broad a range of cultures as possible. Even so, the majority of the prayers given here are to Indo-European, Egyptian, or Wiccan deities, since these are the most common cultures that Neo-Pagans operate in. And I hope I may be excused the personal foible of including some prayers to Proto-Indo-European deities.

I have attempted to remedy this further by writing some prayers to deities assigned by function rather than by name—to hearth deities, storm deities, etc. There are characteristics shared by types of deities in different cultures, so I have written these prayers to line up with the commonalities. Even some of the prayers I've written to particular deities can be adapted to others: Indra fighting the serpent Vṛtra isn't too different from Thor and his opposition to the Midgard serpent.

Other reviewers remarked about the style of the prayers. My natural style is sparse. Some saw that as an advantage, but others found the prayers less moving for it. I'm not about to change my basic style, but for the sake of those who like their prayers more flowery I have written some that are less sparse. I must admit that making the effort to write them was a lot of fun.

The discussion of theory in Part I will raise more questions than it answers. It gives things to think about when writing or performing a prayer rather than instructions on what effect each prayer may have. It is intended as a place to start from, rather than a destination. I have included a bibliography to help point the way onward.

# PART I

# THE FOUNDATIONS
# OF WORSHIP

# CHAPTER 1

# PRAYER

Prayer is communication with some form of the sacred, most often seen as a person or persons. It is a form of speech and, like speech in general, can be divided into marked and unmarked. Unmarked speech is informal. It can be called "conversational," since it is the style we use in conversation. It's a prose style, friendly, using everyday words in everyday arrangement: nothing fancy here. In prayer this style is most appropriate for deities with whom you are on very good terms, and for those who are close to people in general and therefore likely to be friendly to us—for instance hearth goddesses, homey deities who live with us and with whom we interact daily. Prayers to other kinds of beings can be in this style as well; ancestors, who were people like us, may enjoy it, as long as it is respectful. High gods like Zeus, on the other hand, may not appreciate being treated on chummy terms.

Conversational prayers are almost nonexistent among the prayers we have from ancient times. Although this may be due to the vagaries of survival, it may be because these less formal prayers express a theology that sees little distinction between the deities and humans—a belief not common in those times.

For other sorts of prayers, marked speech is most common. Marked speech is simply any form that is out of the ordinary. At one end of this spectrum is elevated prose like "newscasters' speech," in which grammatical niceties are observed, and words more common in written than spoken speech are used. The interest here is clarity and precision rather than decoration. The more formal types of elevated prose include technical terms; a good example is legal speech. Elevated prose may include sentences that have become ritualized: "I now pronounce you husband and wife." It may contain archaic terms like "thou," or words that still exist but are used with archaic meanings, such as "suffer" for "allow." These words are used not just for their basic meanings, but also for their psychological and social implications. Fancy words are seen as expressing fancy thought.

In elevated prose, grammatical rules for word order may be played with—for instance, "For this I pray" rather than "I pray for this." The style may be magisterial, conveying, without actually stating, that the occasion is an important one. Here we see the beginnings of poetry, in which the way something is expressed is as important as its literal meaning.

Elevated prose is often used in speeches. A classic example is the Gettysburg Address, which uses archaic and unusual terms: "four score and seven" is certainly not the common way to express "eighty-seven"; "brought forth" is not likely to be found in everyday speech, and "conceived," at least in the sense that Lincoln used it, is equally uncommon.

These words are carefully chosen and arranged. There is, for instance, a parallelism in the structure of the speech. Something that is "brought forth" is something that has been "conceived." There is the metaphor of the emergence of a country as that of a child. There is connecting structure between sections of the speech: "dedicate" and "consecrate" are repeated, and "who struggle here" is paired with "who fought here." This is not casual speech; it has been carefully crafted to draw listeners in and to make a logical argument. It is beautiful, but its beauty is in service to its purpose.

This sort of speech requires a lot of practice and skill, careful planning and editing, or both. In the case of the Gettysburg Address, it was both; Lincoln had developed his speaking skill in years of legal argument and debate, and, despite the legend, the Address was not dashed off on the back of an envelope on the way to Gettysburg, but went through several drafts. (A wonderful history and for our purposes a very relevant account of this is found in Wills, 1993, 148–175.) I think this would be too much to expect when writing a prayer, at least at first, but it's a good goal.

A very formal type of speech is found in the King James Bible. Contrary to what many think, the language of this translation is not the English spoken at the time of King James. It is consciously archaic, looking back toward Elizabethan England, but formalized to create a language that no one had ever actually spoken. Even at the time of the translation, it was marked. Moreover, the text was designed to be spoken rather than read, so careful attention was paid to flow, ease of pronunciation, and meter (Nicolson, 2003). The end result comes very close to poetry.

And it is poetry that is the most marked form of speech, and it was the most common form for prayers in ancient times. Even many prayers that seem at first to be prose have been shown to be structured like poetry (Watkins, 1995). It's therefore useful to have a good knowledge of how poetry works when you are writing prayers.

## Poetic Structure

It is difficult to define poetry, and the line between it and elevated prose is not always easy to draw. The definition in Wikpedia is "a form of literary art in which language is used for its aesthetic and evocative qualities in addition to, or in lieu of, its apparent meaning." This could be applied to some other forms of elevated prose as well. There are some differences, however; in poetry this definition is more intensely applied. In particular, poetry pays careful attention to beauty; it is decorative. This decoration, however, carries part of the meaning.

Although in recent years the rules governing the type of compositions considered to be poetry have loosened, there are traditional poetic formats. These may limit the number of lines, the meter, and the rhyme scheme. We all know about sonnets and haikus, for instance.

The grossest level of a poem is its overall structure. Is there one verse or more? If there are more than one, are they separated by a chorus? A verse/chorus structure is possible whether a prayer is sung or spoken. In either case it works well in groups, where a main celebrant may sing or say the verse, and everyone joins in on the chorus.

When composing a poem or prayer, you need to decide how many lines you want. If you are using a set format like a sonnet, this may be decided for you. (An English sonnet, for instance, has fourteen lines.) You also need to consider syllable count. Each line can consist of a set number of syllables. (In English sonnets, each line has ten.) Lines may have differing numbers of syllables, however, even in some set formats. The most familiar pattern of this is probably that of the haiku, with three lines in a syllable count of 5-7-5. I am very fond of this form, since it leads to short prayers that are still tightly constructed.

Haikus traditionally present a stripped-down description of nature that is then related to an emotional state or the transcendent, making them very suitable for Pagan prayers. A haiku prayer can end in a call to or praise of a divine being:

★  Winter snow lies thick
    on the frozen ground beneath:
    Hail, Winter Spirits!

The structure can be modified to suit your purpose. For instance, sometimes I use an extended haiku format. Instead of three lines, 5-7-5, I may use 5-7-5-5 or 5-7-5-7:

★  Winter snow lies thick
    on the frozen ground beneath:
    Hail, Winter Spirits!
    Hail all of you here!

Or I may extend the number of syllables in the last line—
5-7-6—or truncate the last line—5-7-4—or combine
extended line length and truncated syllable count—5-7-
5-4—or the reverse:

★  Winter snow lies thick
    on the frozen ground beneath:
    Hail, Winter Spirits!
    Hail in the cold!

A final line with an unexpected number of syllables gives a
strong feeling of completion; it sticks out as important. It
is marked. The suddenness of the shorter line, for instance,
makes the prayer feel complete, concrete. A longer line, on
the other hand, may make you feel as if a new line has
started but been left unfinished; the connection with the
sacred is open. The first is good for a petitionary prayer,
and the second is good for a calling or prayer of praise. Try
them out and see what emotional response each evokes
in you.

Other syllable counts can convey other feelings. Lines
of the same length can create peace and contentment:

★  Winter snow lies thick
    covering the ground.
    Hail, Winter Spirits!

Lengthening or shortening the last line in non-haiku
poems—5-5-6 or 6-6-5—can have an effect similar to their
effect in haikus:

★  Winter snow lies thick
   covering the ground.
   Hail, bright Winter Spirits!

Play around with syllable counts, and they may become the unifying principle of your prayer style.

## Meter and Rhyme

The next level down from syllable count is meter. This is the pattern of long and short syllables, or of accented and unaccented syllables, or of open and closed syllables. These overlap somewhat, with a closed syllable being longer than an open one, and long syllables tending to be accented. (An open syllable is a vowel or one ending with a vowel (V, CV), whereas a closed syllable ends in a consonant (VC, CVC).)

Meter is what drives a poetic line. Does it rush on, or take its time? Does it come smoothly to a stop, or end with a crash?

Meter is a skeleton on which to hang words, which means that the composer is creating order from chaos. This was an important part of ancient religion, so doing it within a prayer makes that prayer into a reflection of one of the goals of religion itself. By composing or speaking structured speech you become a creator of a well-ordered cosmos.

Meter also gives beauty to a prayer. This is in large part due to the response we have to good structure. It may also come from our strong connection to rhythm.

There are a variety of meters, each with a different feel. The famous iambic pentameter, in which each line has five groups of unstressed/stressed combinations of syllables, is a natural meter for English, and is therefore the easiest for us to write and the easiest on our ears. "We wish that you might come to us today." More exotic meters can make a prayer more marked, but also more difficult to write well, with the danger of the language being a bit stilted. For instance, the trochee, which is made up of an accented syllable followed by an unaccented one (the reverse of iambic), may have been the meter followed by the great Finnish epic, the *Kalevala,* but it is also that of "Hiawatha," making it hard for those raised on Longfellow to take seriously.

Repetition within a prayer is similar to meter, giving it a structure around which the rest of the prayer turns. Some parts can be repeated and others not, as in a song with verses and choruses. This gives a combination of order and change that may well express the nature of a deity or aspects of the divine reality in which they operate.

Moreover, each time the repeated part is said, it drives itself deeper into our consciousness, each time modified by the nonrepeated part. These modifying words or phrases in a sense fall into the hole dug by the repetition of the other parts. The truth of the repetition is thus manifested in different ways, increasing your understanding of it.

One kind of prayer that uses repetition is a litany, which consists of a call and response. A main celebrant says one thing; this is answered by the others; the main celebrant says something else; the others answer, and so on. The others can repeat what the celebrant has said, or they can say something different, which is then repeated each time they respond:

★ *Celebrant*: We pray to the one who knows the runes.
  *All*: Odin is he, Odin is wise.
  *Celebrant*: We pray to the one who hears memory's tales.
  *All*: Odin is he, Odin is wise.
  *Celebrant*: We pray to the one who rescued the mead.
  *All*: Odin is he, Odin is wise.

A variation on this is the question-and-answer format:

★ *Celebrant*: Who is the one who gives birth to the world?
  *All*: The Goddess is she, the mother of all.
  *Celebrant*: Who is the one who comforts the ailing?
  *All*: The Goddess is she, the mother of all.
  *Celebrant*: Who is the one who shines in the nighttime?
  *All*: The Goddess is she, the mother of all.

Finally, we come to word choice. All of the considerations of elevated prose apply here—archaisms, alliterations, and so on. These are more important in poetry than in prose. "Thou" sounds silly outside of the most elevated prose, but can fit in well with certain types of poems.

Word choice can follow a pattern. The best-known is rhyme. This is very common in modern poetry—so much so that many incorrectly see it as poetry's defining characteristic. Rhyme was rare in the ancient world, however. A big reason for this is that many ancient languages are highly inflected. This means that the endings of words changed with their use. For instance, the usual Latin ending for a first-person plural verb (the "we" form) was -*mus*. This makes rhyming so easy and boring that there isn't much point in it. In a sense, the endings don't really rhyme, but rather are identical. It is harder to rhyme in modern English, so English rhymes can be both more subtle and more complex, and therefore more marked and more beautiful.

Rhyme schemes are as varied as meters. The easiest rhyme to construct is couplets—two lines that end in the same sound. These couplets are then "stacked" to make a poem in the form "aabbcc", etc.:

★ Demeter, blesser of women and men,
  as was done of old we call you again,
  Holy Queen and Mother of Earth
  bring life, and bring laughter, and birth.

Couplets can become boring in a long prayer, but you can use that to lull the consciousness into an altered state. Couplets can also be used to good effect in litanies, with the response changing each time, but rhyming with the call.

More complicated, but more common, is an "abab" structure, in which the first line rhymes with the third, the second with the fourth, and so on:

★ Demeter, blesser of women and men,
   Queen and Mother of Earth,
   as was done of old we call you again,
   bring life, and bring laughter, and birth.

More complicated schemes exist. For instance, in addition to end rhymes, in which the last syllable of each line rhymes with the last syllable of other lines, there are internal rhymes, where words inside of each line rhyme with those inside of others. One of the prayers in this book contains both end and internal rhymes:

★ With rain, he brings us the greening,
   with grain, he brightens our days,
   with might he drives away falseness,
   with right he opens our ways.

Note that I have combined couplets formed by the internal lines with an "abcb" pattern formed by the end rhymes. This sort of poetry is hard to write, which is one reason why out of the hundreds of prayers in this book there is only one like it.

Shakespeare often used rhymes in an interesting way by ending unrhymed soliloquies with the rhymed words. After a number of unrhymed lines, there is a couplet. Take, for instance, *Henry IV*, Part I, Act I, scene 2, where, after twenty unrhymed lines, we find:

*I'll so offend as to make offense a skill*
*Redeeming time when men think least I will.*

One prayer in this book ends in this way:

★  Know this, then: averting my eyes I still praise;
   I honor with words, though not perhaps my gaze.

Using a couplet in this way can provide a clear ending to
a prayer, without having to carry a rhyme scheme through
the whole prayer. It can be especially useful in groups,
where the couplet can be a good cue that the prayer is
over.

Rhyme has the same advantages as meter. It provides
structure, beauty, and ease of memorization. It also has the
disadvantage of being more difficult to do well. There are
many truly bad rhymed prayers out there. The most common danger is to use clichéd rhymes—the moon-June-
spoon problem. In other instances, the words don't rhyme
exactly: for example, "mine" and "time." An unrhymed
prayer is better than a poorly rhymed one.

Another type of word choice is alliteration, which
occurs when two words begin with the same sound:
"bright and beautiful," "great and glorious," "dewy dawn."
Note that it is the sounds, not the spellings, that create
the alliteration: "carefully" alliterates with "kill," not "celebrate." In some systems, all vowels alliterate, so that "easy"
doesn't alliterate just with "easel," but with "aisle."

Alliteration is the basis of Germanic poetry, which
is made up of lines that are divided in half by a slight
pause:

★  Holy in heaven,                    we hail you, Tyr.

In each half there are two accented syllables, or "lifts." The main lift of the line is the first accented syllable in the second half. One or both of the lifts in the first half of the line must alliterate with it, but the second lift in the second half must not. There is more to Germanic poetic rules (see Tolkien, 2009, 45–50), but this will do for now. I bring this up here because it is a very appropriate style for prayers to Germanic deities, and because it is a natural and powerful style for English.

Synonyms help with word choice. One of the glories of English is its large vocabulary, and this can be used to great advantage in prayer. Synonyms can be useful if you want a word of a particular meter, or are looking for a rhyme, or for a word to alliterate. They rarely have exactly the same meaning, however. Their meanings can overlap in some ways and diverge in others. "Cease" implies a complete ending; "halt" is abrupt (Hayakawa, 1968, 593).

Even if the meanings of synonyms are the same, they often differ in level of formality. English has many synonyms in which one word is Germanic in origin—simple, friendly, everyday—and one is from Latin, French, or Greek—longer, formal, marked. Compare "ask" and "request." Even Germanic words can differ in level of formality; "ask" is a very different word from "beseech."

The use of synonyms in succeeding verses is called parallelism. This is a form of repetition in which it is the idea that's repeated, not the words. For instance:

★  I pray to you for help,
   I ask you for your aid.

In this case, each line has two words that have synonyms in the other. This can even be done with more than three lines:

★　We give praise to the Shining Ones.
　　We honor the High Holy Ones.
　　We worship them as is right.

This example shows how you can combine different techniques for effect. "Give praise to," "honor," and "worship" are parallels that tie the three lines together, as does the number of syllables (eight per line) and the "we" at the beginning of each. The last line differs from the others, however. The first two have a second parallel—"Shining Ones" and "High Holy Ones." This is missing in the final line, replaced by the pronoun "them," which has been shifted toward the beginning. This leaves a hole, into which something new has been dropped—a reason for the action(s). There are two ways this structure can be expressed: 1 / 2 // 1 /2 // 1 / 3, or action//action//action/reason.

In these ways this prayer, short as it is, has been tied together and still provides a clear ending. We've seen the same clear ending in syllable counts and final couplets, and here we see how you can use more than one technique to cap off a prayer.

Other techniques can be used, of course—the two last words can alliterate, for instance. Don't use too many of these techniques at once, however, or the prayer may seem fussy. Don't feel as if you always have to have a hard-hitting end, either. Sometimes a prayer can be effective when it just trails off.

## Poetic Style

Prayers should be beautiful, and there are many ways to achieve that. A prayer can be a gothic cathedral, lacy and strong. It can be a Japanese tea room, sparse and balanced. It can be a Picasso, showing different sides of an idea all at once. Pick a method and stick with it for the length of the prayer. Otherwise you will have a mess on your hands.

There are many other poetic techniques that can be used to good effect in prayers to increase both their beauty and their depth. This book is threatening to become a hand-book on poetry, however, so I will simply recommend that you consult any one of a number of introductions to poetry. Wikipedia's entry on "poetry" is a good place to start.

More important, read poets, especially the greats. You probably read them in school, but read them again. Read Whitman and Frost and Yeats, and yes, Shakespeare too, both his poetry and his prose. Read over your favorites— they're your favorites for a reason. Read other people's poetic prayers, ancient and modern, even non-Pagan ones. *The Book of Common Prayer* is a good source.

While you are reading, allow yourself to absorb. See what turns of phrase are used. Get a feel for how one word flows into another, and for how sentences are ordered. Pay attention to how two words that are supposed to mean the same thing can still feel different.

Immerse yourself in poets, pick up their style, and try to write like them. Write hymns to the Greek gods in the style of the Homeric hymns, and to the Vedic gods in the style of the *Rig Veda*. Don't worry that you aren't being original in this; you are trying on styles to find your own. Try out the styles of modern poets, too. Try to write a prayer like Frost or Yeats, for instance. Eventually you will find a style or styles that appeal to you. You will then find it easy to write in that style and to respond to prayers written in it.

Case in point: J. R. R. Tolkien wrote an extended poem in Germanic alliterative form (Tolkien, 1985). When I was reading it over the course of a few days, I became immersed in the style. As I was planning my day in the shower on one of those days, I realized that I was thinking in the style. Perhaps you won't be influenced to that extent (perhaps you *shouldn't* be), but some transfer will take place, and this will be a step toward developing your own style.

There is no shame in adopting another's style. If it is beautiful, if it speaks to you, then why not? No sense reinventing the wheel. But maybe your survey of other people's styles will lead you to realize that you don't like any of them, and that may lead you to create your own style or styles. Great, go for it.

Do all this and you will find a style that works for you. Do that well enough, and your style will work for others. At the very least, however, do it well enough that it works for the deities to whom it is addressed. Don't be so afraid that your work isn't good enough that you abandon the effort; be just afraid enough to want to write the best prayers you can.

One thing that will help you in this is to remember that prayers are meant to be spoken aloud. You are writing for speech, not for sight. Speak your prayers, either as you compose them or after. You need to learn not only how words fit together, but also how they sound.

Good poetry is easy to say. A good structure keeps the tongue from tripping over words; one follows the other in a natural way. The beauty of structure makes possible a beauty of performance.

This overlaps with another function of specific forms— that they are comfortable by being familiar. For instance, even though the haiku wasn't designed for prayer, its format is well-enough known that the format is comfortable to hear and say.

A nonintuitive function of structured form is that the work involved in creating a prayer can be balanced by the ease with which it can be said. The form does a share of the work. Well-structured prayers, no matter how much sweat has gone into them, can be easier to say than conversational ones.

## Poetic Ideas

So far, we have talked about techniques for arranging words, for giving them a structure. There are also rules and techniques for arranging the ideas in a prayer—for how to structure the prayer as a whole. Writing prayers is made easier by using one of a number of prayer structures. In *A Book of Pagan Prayer*, I discussed one of them.

In this form, you begin by identifying the deity addressed. This can be done in one or more ways: by name, by title, or by relating a myth: "Indra, Killer of Vṛtra, who freed the cows." Titles can express different sides of a deity. Is Brighid "inspirer of poets," "goddess of the hearth," or "provider of sustenance"? She is all of these, and a praise of her that mentions them all may be the better for it. Titles can also be used in a limiting way, to specify which aspect of the deity is being called upon—a kind of "heads-up" as to the request that is coming up. "Mars who guards my field" is subtly different from "Mars who guards our armies."

Next comes praise. The relation of a myth may be considered praise, but something more explicit is commonly used. Titles often convey praise: "Bull of a thousand cows, warrior of unconquerable strength."

This is followed by a reminder of what the worshipper has done for the deity in the past and vice versa: "To whom I have many times offered butter, offered foaming drinks, who has been my protector and aid in struggles past." This establishes that the worshipper and the deity already have a relationship; one does favors for friends.

This may overlap and slide into reasons why the deity should grant the request. This can include favors done by the deity in the past, with the assumption that they'll be willing to perform them again, and a reminder that the request is within the area of the deity's function.

Then comes the current request: "I ask of you further protection, further aid, further support in today's confrontation." Note the parallels in our developing prayer.

Words are repeated from previous lines ("protect," "aid")
or replaced with synonyms ("struggles," "confrontation").
There is also augmentation, perhaps to suggest that this
request is a continuation of past gifts, or to drive the prayer
forward: "protect" and "aid" becomes "protect," "aid," and
"support." The petition can be in the form of a request:
"May you grant this." Or, oddly enough, it may be spoken
as a command: "Grant this."

The prayer is finished with a promise or vow. It
may be general: "I will always have reason to remember and praise you." Or it may be more specific: "Well-
protected, I will offer you butter, burned in the fire, after
my victory."

The final prayer reads like this:

★   Indra, Killer of Vṛtra, who freed the cows,
      Bull of a thousand cows, warrior of unconquerable
            strength,
       to whom I have many times offered butter, offered
            foaming drinks,
      who has been my protector and aid in struggles past:
      I ask of you further protection, further aid, further
            support in today's confrontation.
      Well-protected, I will offer to you butter, burned in
            the fire, after my victory.

This is the standard structure of prayers to Indo-European
deities, those of most of the cultures from Europe to India,
and it is a good one to use in general. Other cultures have

other traditional structures. Typical Egyptian prayers, for instance (Redford, 2002, 313–4), are structured like this:

First is praise, often with many titles: "Isis, throne of kings, mother of gods and men, whose name was praised in Egypt and Rome."

Then comes a description of the one praying, often self-deprecating: "I who am poor in goods, and weak in power, and in need of aid, pray to you."

Next, a mention of a specific transgression, especially if it is seen as having caused the problem the prayer is about: "I, who in my weakness have violated the commands of heaven."

Then follows the request, especially in terms of the violation: "I who am weak from transgressing the holy way, who have become ill from my transgression, ask for healing from the disease I suffer."

Now comes a promise of future praise, especially in a public way: "I who have prayed to you will make your power well-known to those I encounter."

Finally, there is a description of the request as if already granted: "I say this, I who have been healed by you, Isis, queen of heaven."

So we have:

★ Isis, throne of kings, mother of gods and men,
    whose name was praised in Egypt and Rome,
    I, who am poor in goods, and weak in power, and in
        need of aid, pray to you,

I, who in my weakness have violated the commands
    of heaven,
I, who am weak from transgressing the holy way,
    who have become ill from my transgression, ask
    for healing from the disease I suffer.
I, who have prayed to you will make your power
    well-known to those I encounter.
I say this, I who have been healed by you, by Isis,
    queen of heaven.

A different structure used to address the *kami*, beings or
things of sacred power, is found in Shintoism (Nelson,
1996, 108–13):

A call to those present: "You who have gathered here to
pray to these kami on this day, hear me."

A statement of purpose: "I pray that all might be made
as pure as it is proper to be, as it is proper to do."

An historical precedent, expressed as a myth: "As it
was indeed pure when the land was made. It was then that
Izanagi no Mikoto and Izanami no Mikoto formed it. Then
the spear was dipped in the sea, stirred it into foam; then
from the foam came the land, pure and shining."

The reason the prayer is required: "Yet we have done
impure deeds. We have broken divine laws. We have violated familial obligations. We have supported the wrong."

A description of what is to be done: "When these are
done, the people pour out sake, they dance in the ancient
way to please the kami. Best of all things, and before these

things, they purify themselves, washing in pure water. They wash the hands which offer, they wash the mouth that prays."

Next, the way the kami will respond: "With our purification of ourselves, the kami will be inspired to purify perfectly. With the performance of proper rites, the kami will be inspired to purify all. Izanagi no Mikoto and Izanimi no Mokito will impart the purity of the new land to each and to all, for now and for the future."

Finally, an ending: "This is what I say today."

And so:

★ You who have gathered here to pray to these kami on this day, hear me.

I pray that all might be made as pure as it is proper to be, as it is proper to do; as it was indeed pure when the land was made.

It was then that Izanagi no Mikoto and Izanami no Mikoto formed it. Then the spear was dipped in the sea, stirred it into foam; then from the foam came the land, pure and shining.

Yet we have done impure deeds. We have broken divine laws. We have violated familial obligations. We have supported the wrong.

When these are done, the people pour out sake, they dance in the ancient way to please the kami. Best of all things, and before these things,

they purify themselves, washing in pure water.
They wash the hands that offer, they wash the
mouth that prays.
With our purification of ourselves, the kami will be
inspired to purify perfectly. With the performance of proper rites, the kami will be inspired
to purify all. Izanagi no Mikoto and Izanimi no
Mokito will impart the purity of the new land to
each and to all, for now and for the future.
This is what I say today.

There are other formats as well. One I often use is to go from the mundane to the sacred. First I describe the situation: the season has changed, I am sick, I lack inspiration. I then bring to mind a deity or an aspect of divine reality with which this may be linked by myth, function, or imagery. This gives the situation sacred meaning; I link the present with the eternal. In a sense, it's like a haiku.

This is enough for praise or for observance of an occasion. For petitions, however, once I have connected the situation with a deity and gained contact with someone from whom I can ask a favor, I add a line or two expressing that.

The basic idea behind all these forms is the same, however: name the deity, make the request, state why the deity should respond, state what the worshipper will give in return. The order of the elements may vary, as well as their content, but these are the core concepts found in most prayers.

It's a good thing if a prayer has an obvious end. This can be shown as simply as by a drop in your tone of voice. It can also be written into the prayer itself, as in the Shakespearian couplet.

Those who grew up in a Christian or Wiccan environment may feel that a prayer is unfinished without an "Amen" or "So mote it be." This kind of ending can be in the language of the person praying (e.g., "So be it") or the language associated with the deity prayed to (e.g., "Bíodh sé amhlaidh" for an Irish deity).

As we have seen, this can be especially useful in group rituals, where these words can be an affirmation by the group of what has been prayed by a particular person. It can be used as a punctuation point, separating prayers in a ritual. It can be used more than once in a prayer, as if one prayer were piled on another. If you do this, however, make sure the final ending phrase is more emphatic—by saying it more than once, for instance. A final line may be more elaborate, to put a seal on the prayer: "May it be so, may it be so, may it truly be so."

I've spoken several times about beauty. That a prayer be beautiful is important for a number of reasons. One comes from the deities being individuals. They have free will, they have preferences. They are therefore more likely to be favorable toward those who please them, and beauty is pleasing.

Moreover, a cosmos is organized by aesthetic principles. A poorly constructed and performed prayer is like swimming against a stream, while a beautiful one has the power of the cosmos behind it; it is in accord with the way the cosmos works. It is in tune with the cosmos, and thus more in touch with the sacred. The more in tune with the cosmos you are, the easier it will be for the gods to grant your desires.

Also, when you are praying in praise of someone (e.g., a deity) or something (e.g., a season), the prayer should reflect that someone or something. It is part of Pagan theology that the sacred is beautiful (even when it is a terrible beauty), so a beautiful prayer will express in words what is actually going on. Finally, a beautiful prayer has an effect on the one praying. This is especially important in prayers praising deities or honoring seasons—the beauty of the prayer imprints the beauty of the target or occasion.

## Prayer and Music

Prayer, like all forms of communication, is not just about words. The way in which prayers are presented can also be marked. Prayers are often sung or accompanied by music, even if only by a drum. You can use the musical style both to create a mood and to conform to the culture of the deity addressed—Irish music for an Irish deity, Vedic chanting for a Vedic one. Gregorian chants, even though originating in a monotheistic tradition, have become identified in our minds with praise and quiet devotion, and so can be useful. I myself would like to see fewer pseudo-Celtic songs and fewer minor keys in modern Paganism. Experiment with Country and Western, Blues, Rock, Rap. Pagans are supposed to be creative. Create.

Don't abandon minor keys completely, however. These can be great for meditations, since their droning can calm the mind. They are also appropriate for chthonic deities, or for the dead.

Major keys are brighter, lighter, happier. (They are also easier to sing.) They would be more appropriate for the brighter deities like sky gods, or happy occasions like weddings or the spring.

Time signatures are the musical equivalent of meters. In fact, it is difficult to write music for a prayer that doesn't have a meter, or at least a syllabic structure. One way to fill out the lines of a nonsyllabic prayer so it can be sung is with grace notes—a single syllable getting more than one note. This is very common in Gregorian chants, Irish *sean-nós*, and Arabic singing, among other forms.

Each time signature has its own effect: 4/4 is the most comfortable to sing; 2/2 drives on; 3/4 is a waltz and therefore easily associated with elegance, and so on. Unusual meters like 6/8 are difficult to sing, so they are best kept to solitary rituals, but they have their own uses.

These are Western rhythms, of course. If you are worshipping deities from non-Western cultures you may want to look at their rhythms—the pulsing beat of many American Indian songs, poly-rhythms from Africa, rhythms in seven time from the Balkans. Or you may just want to stick to rhythms that you can do easily. Better a non–culturally specific rhythm done well than a poor performance of a culturally specific one.

Your choice of instruments may also have meaning. We all connect bagpipes with Celtic music, especially Scottish music, for instance. But they're found in other regions

as well, and their mournful wail is worth experiment-
ing with. Flutes are found in both Roman and American
Indian rituals, giving them a cross-cultural character. This
is true of many instruments.

The simplest and most common type of instrument is
percussion. Certain types of these are also associated with
certain cultures—*bodhrans* with Ireland, slit drums with
Polynesia. They can be used to line up with the meter of a
spoken prayer.

Partway between poetry and music is chanting, which
uses a small number of notes, sometimes as few as two. An
effective chant requires or creates a strong rhythm. Chants
are usually short and are very useful in groups, where the
rhythm makes it easy to pray in unison. Chants are often
repeated a number of times, which makes them great for
guests, since they can pick up a chant as it goes along.

## Gestures and Positions

All forms of communication have characteristics that are
nonverbal (and nonmusical). These include tone of voice,
facial expressions, and body positions, especially of the
hands. I won't go into all of them deeply here, just give an
overview of body positions and encourage you to experiment with all ways to express an idea.

It's easy to think of body positions traditionally associated with praying. Standing, kneeling, prostration, and the
many positions of yoga are among those that have been
used by Pagans. One is so connected with prayer that it is
called the *orans* ("praying") position. In this position, the

arms are held out at a 90-degree angle to the body, then bent up at the elbow in another 90-degree angle, with the palms open to the front. I don't know the meaning or origin of this position, but it is widespread. Perhaps it is like many greetings—a way of showing you are unarmed—or perhaps it is a sign of openness.

Hand and arm positions are also important. The Hindu *mudras* are fairly well-known; less familiar are those of Thai dancing, which can tell a story just as words do. It would be interesting to compose a prayer in sign language, performing it either on its own or accompanied by spoken words. Sign language has its own rules of poetry that could be played with.

These forms of gestures are mostly arbitrary. There are more natural ones, such as holding out cupped hands as a sign of giving. There are also gestures that have been absorbed so strongly from culture that they are automatic and comfortable—like shaking hands, which might be very interesting to use in a prayer of coming together.

Positions aren't always static, either. There are times when you may take a position, perhaps extending your arms, and hold it for the whole prayer. At other times, you may change positions, perhaps starting with your hands close to your body, then thrusting them forward as an act of giving as you speak your intent, then bringing them in toward your chest as if receiving what you prayed for. Gestures can serve as words, paralleling or supplementing what is spoken, with their arrangement serving like the structure of a sentence. The flow between them is just one more thing to play with to achieve maximum meaning and beauty.

Pressed further, changing gestures become dance. Dance can be a prayer in and of itself, an expression of emotions, an offering of beauty, a form of nonverbal communication. Dance does not lend itself well to spoken prayers, but prayers recited silently while dancing can be effective. In group prayers, one or more people can dance while prayers are spoken or sung by others. Alternatively, one person can say a prayer while everyone else dances. Very simple dances can work with simple chants.

## Performance

Prayers can be spontaneous, read, or memorized. There is a certain bias among modern Pagans toward spontaneous prayers. We are supposed to be creative and inspired. The feeling is that if we "speak from the heart" all will be well. To be perfectly frank, however, we aren't more creative than most people until we have trained ourselves to be. I'm sure we have all suffered through halting performances of rambling spontaneous prayers from people "speaking from the heart."

As you write and perform more and more prayers, you will get better at spontaneous praying, just as jazz musicians first learn their scales and then learn to improvise. I'm not saying that your early spontaneous prayers will be ineffective (out of tune). They may simply be less beautiful and less precise than those you may eventually be able to compose. But I am *definitely* saying that, to be good at improvising, you need to learn your scales.

Previously written prayers can be memorized or read, and may be written by yourself or by others. Besides being easier to write well (editing is a wonderful thing), prepared prayers allow you to concentrate on performance rather than production. This allows you to think about tone of voice, pauses, gestures, and other stylistic touches that add to the beauty of the performance. Don't underestimate the value of preplanning and rehearsing these touches.

Some people have problems memorizing. I know my own memorization skills have decreased over time. Someone reciting an insufficiently memorized prayer will stumble over words, pause at inappropriate points to remember, go back to forgotten points automatically, or without thinking say, "wait," before redoing a poorly recited part. A poorly memorized prayer isn't as good as one read well.

Reading prayers is okay, and even expected on certain occasions. Weddings and funerals that are attended by non-Pagans are examples. We have become so used to an officiant reading from a book that people may take a memorized prayer less seriously (and a spontaneous one not seriously at all). It is very important to read a prayer over a few times before the ritual to become familiar with it. Otherwise you may find yourself tripping over the words.

One of the great strengths of prepared prayers is that they can be repeated, which can have great psychological effects. It's especially nice for prayers for comfort; familiarity can bring peace all on its own. Also, each time a prayer is said you may discover new meanings in it, new connections with the divine, new understandings of the deity you are addressing. This can be true even if you have written the prayer yourself. You may have touched on an aspect of the divine you had not understood, but which now, through the continued reflection brought about by repetition, becomes clear to you.

This is one of the functions of the extreme form of repetition known as mantras. These are prayers, usually short (sometimes just the name of a deity, even a single syllable) repeated many times, usually rhythmically, sometimes with motions like rocking to bring the words into the body. Mantras are also chanted, or even sung. They may be petitions or they may be meant to reinforce either some aspect of the cosmos or one's connection with it: "Peace, peace, peace." They may also function well as praise: "Glory to Gaṇeśa."

In some traditions, such as Hinduism (whence the word "mantra," meaning "tool for thought," comes), the literal meaning of the words may not be thought to matter. It is instead the sound that is thought to reflect divine reality in some way. An extreme form of this is found in Zoroastrianism, where one and a half hours of a two-hour *yasna* ritual is taken up by chanting in Avestan, a language incompletely known to the priests, and even somewhat opaque to modern linguists. A mantra like this is extremely difficult to write, however; the connection between sound and the sacred was worked out over millennia by many people. You are unlikely to stumble upon one in the course of your prayer writing. If you want to use a mantra in this way, I recommend working with one already developed/discovered.

## Offerings and Sacrifice

Prayers are often accompanied by offerings. These have traditionally included animal sacrifices, libations, food, incense, and just about anything else. Because of its importance in ancient times and because what is subtle in other kinds of offerings is clear in it, I will begin with sacrifice.

The why of sacrifice has been argued over by scholars for many years with no resolution. I think one reason for this is that scholars have seen sacrifice through the lens of their own ideology, the culture they've studied the most, or their own culture. A Freudian will find a Freudian meaning, an anthropologist who spent his career studying the Nuer will apply Nuer theology, and a member of PETA will find the whole thing offensive.

But the real problem is that they tend to view sacrifice as a single thing. It is one only in the sense that a raised hand is one thing. Is it raised in greeting? To strike? To swear an oath? There is no one meaning to an upraised hand, and there is no one meaning to sacrifice; there are several.

One of these is that something is being given to the sacred. This is the origin of the word "sacrifice," which means to "make sacred." This is usually seen as giving something up, and that's how we tend to use the word in everyday speech. A religious sacrifice, however, is not so much a giving *up* as a giving *to*. It isn't, "aren't I great for depriving myself," but "isn't it great that the deities are getting what they want?"

The giving by ancient Pagans was not one-sided, however. Just as people gave gifts to the deities, so the deities were expected to give some back.

Something like this on a human scale was found in many societies, such as early Germanic ones. There, warriors gave service to their chieftains, who in turn gave them riches, to the point where "ring-giver" became a kenning for "chieftain." A significant aspect of this is that the socially superior person was expected to give more than he or she received. This was how they maintained their status, and was a form of *noblesse oblige*.

This operated on the divine scale, too. The deities were seen as superior, and were therefore expected to return more than what was offered. The sacrifice of a single ram might be expected to increase the fertility of an entire flock. This theory could lead to a certain amount of "manipulation" of the deities by varying the size of the offering. If a single bull was expected to bring certain blessings, how much more would the Greek *hecatomb*, in which 100 animals were sacrificed? A certain one-upsmanship was initiated, in which the gods, because of their superior status, would give greater gifts than they received.

This is sacrifice in terms of reciprocity and hospitality. These can be seen as the bases for all relationships. Bonds are established and maintained through reciprocal giving. We have preserved some of the ancient rules of hospitality in our own culture. I invite you to my house for dinner, and now you have an obligation to invite me to yours. If I'm always the one doing the inviting, our chance for friendship will fizzle out.

It's the same with the gods. We offer to them, and the gods have a social obligation to repay us. Since they can't invite us over for dinner, they repay our invitation in other ways: prosperity, health, success, etc. By this exchange we become friends with the gods.

This leads us to another meaning of sacrifice, a shared meal. Part of the sacrifice was burned as the gods' share. This was sometimes symbolically important parts of the animal like the heart. It usually included fat and bones.

The gods' share may seem poor, consisting primarily of the inedible portion, as if we were giving them trash. But the gods had their own food. What delighted them was the smoke of the sacrifice. And what parts of the animal burn best? The fat and the bones. The lesson here is that what you serve your guest isn't what *you* like; it's what *they* like.

The other parts were cooked and eaten by the worshipper. The result was a sacred barbecue. It was a shared meal to which the gods were invited, obligating them to return the favor. Sometimes it was the other way round; the gods had already given good things, putting the obligation of reciprocity on the recipients, so the worshippers were throwing a thank-you party in their honor.

Yet another reason the ancients performed sacrifice was the belief that it strengthened the gods. The gods literally fed on the sacrifice, either the smoke or the accompanying prayers. This belief was widespread, found in the

Indo-European world and the Near East, for instance. The gods in some way required people. This implies a very close reciprocal relationship.

Often the important part of this kind of sacrifice was the blood. After all, there is the saying that "blood is life." That is perhaps why in some cultures the blood was poured out on the altar as a libation of sorts, an offering of life to increase the life power of the gods.

Worldwide, offerings to the Dead and to those associated with death (maleficent spirits, and sometimes those connected with the earth) were usually given over completely. We don't *want* to be connected intimately with these spirits, except perhaps on one feast day of the Dead each year, after which they are sent on their way.

Sacrifices are not generally practical these days except for Pagan farmers. If nothing else, they create bad press. This is a shame, but understandable. People think that sacrifice is obsolete, and that killing in honor of a deity is distasteful. There is also a concern for the suffering of the animal. But why should a religious practice become obsolete? *How* could a religious practice become obsolete? If the gods aren't obsolete, why should one of their favorite forms of worship be?

People have become distant enough from the sources of their food that killing seems distasteful. It is certainly not something we use to honor someone. This is not a new idea; it was found in numerous Pagan societies, and led to the abandonment of sacrifice in some. I would ask, however, how honoring it is to an animal to use its meat but deny its death. And can beings as tied up with life and death as the deities are find death distasteful?

In fact, it's the belief that sacrificed animals suffered that is the real problem. And that belief is flat wrong. Although it may be legitimate to be bothered by the animal's death, it was vital in the ancient world that the animal not suffer. In fact, if the animal showed any distress it could not be sacrificed, and if it suffered the sacrifice didn't count. An ancient sacrificial animal was shown far more consideration and suffered far less distress than animals in modern slaughterhouses. Such a sacrifice should arouse no more distaste than *kosher* or *halaal* butchering, and far less than the unsanctified way in which most food animals are slaughtered. Nonetheless, we find ourselves where we find ourselves.

Since so many ancient deities were fond of sacrifices, it is good to do them; since modern sensibilities may be offended by sacrifices, it is good *not* to do them. There is a way out of this dilemma, however, a way that has been used by Pagans both ancient and modern—the use of symbolic substitutes. Something else is named an animal and then treated as one.

Bread has always been the most common substitute. Under the influence of vegetarian Hinduism, for instance, Zoroastrians in India took the bread and butter that had accompanied sacrifices (Jamaspasa, 1985) and used it to replace the sacrifice itself (Modi, 1922, 296–8). A modern example is the replacement of goats with rice wrapped in banana leaves in a 1975 celebration of the Vedic *agnicayana* ritual (Staal, 1983, II:464–5).

Bread can be indentified more closely with an animal by forming it into an animal shape. Baking pans in animal shapes are available for use as molds for forming bread, or as a way to make a cake (another possible substitute) in the proper shape.

Other substitutes are possible, and were made in ancient times as well, possibly by those unable to afford an actual animal. Clay animals have been found in ritual contexts, and make good sacrifices. They do, however, make sharing with the deities impossible. A piece of meat taken from a meal is another possibility. Butter is a great substitute for cattle—it comes from cows, can be part of a shared meal, and burns well. Melted clarified butter is a beautiful thing.

I don't want to give the impression that animal sacrifice is the most common form of offering. Traditionally, the libation was the most common. The Greeks, for instance, poured a libation before drinking anything. You can see here one of the meanings of sacrifice—the shared meal.

Libations are accordingly the most common form of offering you'll see here. They can be of any drink, although alcoholic ones and milk are the most traditional, and certain deities may prefer certain ones. For instance, a goddess connected with cows, such as Brighid, may prefer milk, whereas deities from Egypt, where beer was an important part of the diet, may like that. Here is another meaning of sacrifice; both milk and alcoholic beverages are offerings of life.

Distilled drinks make especially good offerings into fire, since they burn so well. If you use them, however, be careful; they flare up suddenly. (I once came close to a nasty accident with Drambuie.) Butter burns well, as do oils, and are far less dangerous.

Don't pour anything with a low alcohol content or with none at all (milk, for example) directly onto a fire. It will put the fire out—never a good thing in a ritual. Instead, pour it at the base of the fire.

Bread isn't just a good animal substitute, but a worthy offering in itself. It is the "staff of life," a representative of food in general. By sharing it with the divine beings, we are therefore sharing part of all our meals. Bread burns pretty well, too, especially when it has been buttered.

Some offerings can't be burned or poured. No problem; coins can be cast into rivers, jewelry can be buried, etc. Here we find another meaning of sacrifice, giving something over to the gods.

Do you see now why I began my discussion of offerings with sacrifice? Its meanings reverberate throughout other forms. What applies to sacrifice applies to all other offerings, with the appropriate changes.

There are many other kinds of offerings as well. The only requirement is that your offering be seen as valuable to the being to whom it is offered. I've included an appendix with general advice on the kinds of offerings appropriate to various deities, but each will have their own preferences. These can only be found out by research and/ or experimentation.

Of course, a prayer of praise can be an offering as well. In fact, it always is, and the more beautiful the better.

By now you may be thinking that every single thing about a prayer makes a difference. Good; that is the impression I *meant* to give. Prose or poem, meter, word choice, structure, gestures, movements, music, types of offerings—these all matter. Different choices will give different results.

Your choices reverberate on several levels. They will affect you psychologically, putting your mind into a certain frame to receive the presence of the deities. A prayer in an ancient and appropriate style will evoke thought categories associated with a certain culture.

On the theological level, certain styles may appeal to certain deities. Norse deities were used to being addressed with alliterative verse, Semitic with parallel imagery, etc. Praying in these forms can therefore be expected to strike them as pretty and to please them—something desirable in praises, but also when asking for a favor.

Philosophically, doing the thing appropriate for a given situation is an act of beauty. Joining the right words with the right gesture with the right music creates an even higher form of beauty. Yes, that word again—"beauty." If you give the gods nothing else, give them beauty.

# CHAPTER 2

# RITUAL

Pagans, both ancient and modern, have always been fond of ritual. This reflects a major characteristic of Paganism—that what is done is more important than what is believed. That was at once ancient Paganism's greatest weakness and its greatest strength. Because people wanted to perform the best rituals they could, rituals became so complex the average person could neither understand them nor afford to have them celebrated. An emphasis on performance could lead to an empty formalism, with rituals so lacking in emotional appeal that people looked for other ways to satisfy their spiritual desires.

On the other hand, ancient Paganism allowed for more tolerance than belief-centered religion, because it didn't care about what went on inside its practitioners' heads. If practiced correctly, however, ritual-centered religions can be more powerful than creedal ones both at changing beliefs and influencing future actions. That actions change beliefs better than beliefs change actions has been known at least since Aristotle, and expressed since then by such luminaries as Shakespeare and Dr. Phil.

It's difficult to define "ritual." Anthropologists have come up with many definitions, none satisfactory for everything that people look at and say, "Yep, that's a ritual." It comes down more to "I knows 'em when I sees 'em."

Still, I should probably make an attempt at definition. I would say that a ritual is a structured sequence of symbolic actions, words, and objects that from the point of view of a performer at the time of performance are believed to be real, not symbolic. It is therefore wrong to take a tool that outside the ritual symbolizes, for example, air, and inside the ritual say, "With this symbol of Air, I call the element of Air into my ritual space." Rather, you should say: "With this tool of air, I call the element of Air into my ritual space." If the first is done, the element is symbolically present, but with the second it is *really* there.

This has a great effect on the prayers you use in your rituals. Remember to write your prayers and rituals with confidence, speaking your intent into existence. Outside the ritual, weave together symbols; inside the ritual, create reality. If you don't create reality in a ritual, how can you expect it to manifest when you are done? This is, in fact, the theory behind the use of sacrificial substitutes. A loaf of bread offered with the words "This goat to Thor," is, for the time of the ritual, *really* a goat.

As we will see in Part II, there are many types of rituals, and rituals can have many purposes. There are rituals of praise, celebrations of life events, celebrations of seasons, and so on, and there are there are rituals for healing, inspiration, safety, etc. I have not exhausted all the possible purposes of ritual, which are as varied as people's relationships with the sacred and with each other. I hope that the prayers I've written for those I've covered can serve as models for those I haven't.

Ritual, as I'm using the term here, is more appropriate for groups than single prayers are. It would be odd to gather a number of people together to say one prayer, and then be done. At the very least, there should be something that says, "OK, we're here," and another that says, "OK, we're done."

This does not mean that a complete ritual can't be done by an individual. That's done all the time. It's just that rituals consisting of a single prayer are not common.

Some of the prayers in Part II are written just for groups. You don't need a prayer calling people together if there's only one person, and you need at least two people for a wedding. Others, such as the seasonal prayers, can quite easily be used by individuals.

## Ritual Structure

The way the prayers in a ritual are put together, the ritual's structure, is even more important than the prayers themselves. Without structure you have chaos, and a ritual that is chaotic creates chaos in the rest of your life. Furthermore, a structure increases your understanding of a ritual's purpose as it unfolds. Different purposes may require different structures. However, there is a structure shared by many rituals, one that is almost as obvious as Aristotle's beginning-middle-end for stories, and that follows that pattern as well.

First the participants, if there are more than one, need to gather at the place where the ritual will be held. This often involves a procession, which is usually accompanied by singing, music, or at least a drumbeat. Since it is hard to speak in unison while walking, I haven't included any processional prayers here. Alternatively, people can just gather at the ritual site as they show up. This is especially common with either small or very large groups, and with permanent ritual spaces.

Whether people arrive on their own or after a procession, a ritual needs a clear-cut beginning. Even if it begins with a procession, there needs to be something to start the procession. This can be a musical signal like a drum or gong, but that will usually be followed by a prayer.

Opening prayers have two purposes. First, they bring people together, acknowledging that a ritual has begun and that everyone is there for it. Second, they announce the purpose of the ritual. Is it to present a petition? To celebrate a point in life? Simply to worship?

Once a ritual has begun, the participants must be prepared for the sacred. (This can also be done before a procession.) The usual way to do this is through purification. This was very important in ancient times, and is still important today for most modern Pagans. The bowl of water outside an ancient Greek temple and the water source outside a modern Shinto shrine serve the same purpose.

Although washing is the most common method of purification, sometimes what was necessary was time, or things done, or things not done. For example, inscriptions outside Greek temples give rules for how much time after intercourse, giving birth, or being connected with death had to pass before a person was pure enough to enter. Before a ritual, it's good to ask yourself: "Is there any rea-

son why I shouldn't do this? And if so, how can I fix that?"
This question is, in itself, a prayer, and its resolution may
be one as well.

There are a variety of reasons for purification. It provides a clear distinction between the sacred and the mundane. It also provides a sense that what is to be done is
important. It clears the mind of previous concerns.

Theologically, the split between the sacred and the
mundane is the main point. The two are seen as different,
and purification separates the two. It may seem to some
that this insults nature by downgrading the everyday. It's
been found in Paganism from ancient times, however, so
there must be something that is right with it.

The major purpose, I think, is that the ritual be just
what it is. A weed is a plant that, however nice somewhere
else, doesn't belong where it is. The things we need to be
purified of are those that don't belong in a ritual. Purification makes a ritual a garden.

Rituals are often performed in sacred space. The most
basic requirement for sacred space is that it be set apart
in some way. The creation of sacred space is therefore like
purification (and often parts of it include purification). It
makes a place fit for the divine to enter.

A permanent sacred place can be a temple or a cave, or
something as simple as the space surrounding a sacred tree
or stone. Permanent sacred space was the most common
kind in antiquity.

Modern Pagans, however, most commonly worship
in temporary sacred spaces. This is largely an inheritance

from ceremonial magic, where a properly created magic circle is very important. There are practical concerns as well, however. Few modern Pagan groups are wealthy enough to build temples. Some ancient Pagans also used temporary sacred space—the sacred sheds created for Vedic rituals were burned after the ceremonies were completed.

Sacred space is often a representation of a cosmic plan. The idea is to place yourself in a "perfectly" constructed universe that corresponds to a symbolic one in a way that the everyday universe does not. The ritual space thus established corresponds to a sacred plan and thereby becomes sacred.

This cosmos can be created in several ways. It can be declared to exist: "Here in the East are the powers of Air." It can be called into existence directly: "May this stone be the mountain at the center of the world." Or it can be invoked indirectly: "Spirits who dwell in this dark lake, open the ways to the darkness that lurks at the root of all." It can also be brought into being the way the cosmos was brought into being—for instance, with words, by telling a creation myth, or with actions, such as through the repetition of the original sacrifice.

By purification and the creation of a sacred space, you prepare yourself and where you are for the presence of the divine beings. The next step is to call to them. This will, of course, include sentences like, "I call to you," "I ask for your presence," "Come to us." The being called will have to be identified—by name, by title, by the telling of a myth, or by some combination of these.

Calling through titles and myths leads naturally into praise prayers, since relating a myth with respect is a good way to praise a deity, as is the recognition of a deity's characteristics by listing titles. Still, there is always room for "I praise you."

By now you have probably noticed that we are following the classic prayer structure. That's because a prayer can be thought of as a ritual in miniature. Likewise, a ritual can be seen as an unpacked prayer.

Just as in a prayer, a ritual now moves on to its purpose (assuming it wasn't intended simply to praise). Is it a ritual of healing? A seasonal celebration? A rite of passage?

Once the purpose has been fulfilled, or at least prayed for, the ritual winds down, in reverse order. Callings and praise become giving thanks and farewells, the creation of sacred space becomes its dissolution, prayers of coming together become prayers of separation. There is no ritual of de-purification; that will happen soon enough on its own. Some Wiccans "ground and center" at the end of a ritual to drain away magic power and return to the mundane world. This involves meditation and magic more than prayer, so I won't deal with it here, except to note that the prayers for dissolution of sacred space and of separation can be used as part of it.

That's a basic ritual, then: the sacred is created through calling together, purification, creating sacred space, and calling and praising the divine beings (the beginning); the purpose of the ritual is carried out (the middle); things are returned to a mundane condition (the end). Hopefully, the return isn't to an unchanged world, or to an unchanged person.

Some other things that have been said about prayers apply to fuller ritual as well: the importance of the non-verbal; the difference between spontaneous, memorized, and read practices; the usefulness of repetition; and the importance of beauty and organization. And rituals are, of course, made up of prayers.

## Building a Ritual

When you are saying a prayer by yourself, you can choose or write one in whatever style calls to you—or more important, in whatever style you think will appeal to the Holy Ones. In rituals, you don't have as much flexibility. Because they are linked together, the prayers in a ritual interact with each other, so their styles can harmonize or clash.

When you're putting a ritual together, ask yourself how the style of each section fits with the others. Do you want them all in the same style to create a unity? Do you want them to differ so as to provide a strong break between parts? Do you want to start in a relatively everyday style and build up to a very poetic one before winding down again? If you are invoking more than one deity, do you want to have each section in a particular style appropriate to that deity? Do you want to use the same style, with variations only for each deity? The important thing here is that the structure of styles be for a purpose.

There are differences between individual and group rituals. Because there is more than one person, communication is not just with the divine, but also with the human. What is being done should be clear to all. (I say "should" rather than "must" because there is a time and a place for mystery.)

It's because of this that gestures, movements, and objects become more important for groups than they are for individuals. They carry part of the meaning; they are forms of nonverbal communication. This is especially true for motions and gestures. Choreography, taken in its widest sense to include the arrangement and performance of all movements and gestures and the manipulation of tools, is extremely important in group ritual. As with the connection of words, the structure created by connecting motions should be meaningful and beautiful.

At the very least, the motions must not be clumsy. The most basic concern is that people not bump into each other. This sounds simple, but can be surprisingly difficult. Two people are making libations onto a fire, one after another. If they start on the same side of the fire, they will have to pass each other. This can result in awkward maneuvering. It is better if they start on opposite sides. But maybe they have things to do together at another point. Or perhaps there is a fire-tender on one side, blocking access. They will need to know how to approach the fire and then leave without colliding.

A difficulty that can arise even in solitary rituals is the manipulation of objects. Most important is to remember that you only have two hands. You'd be amazed how easy it is to forget that when writing a ritual.

To avoid clumsy fumbling, always put objects in a place that will make them easy to get to at the right time. If two people are to use the same tool at different times, where should it be placed? And where should the participants stand so they don't bump into each other on the way to or from it?

A given tool won't be used after a particular point in the ritual. What should happen to it after that? You don't want to mix it in with tools that you'll be using. A pitcher or bowl with the remains of an offering can be unsightly. Maybe there can be a spot for used tools. Or maybe they can be moved from the side of the space where they began to the other.

A particularly difficult maneuver is the transfer of tools from one person to another. This is especially true of pitchers. If two people need to pour a libation from the same pitcher, there has to be a handoff. Since pitchers are held by the handle, it can be awkward to switch them to another set of hands. The pitcher may even be dropped.

If people start out at a distance from each other, there may be time to put a tool down between their using them. Even if the people start out near each other, this can still be done to smooth out the transfer, with the first person putting the tool down and returning to his or her place before the second comes to get it. This will affect the pacing of the ritual, which is something to keep in mind.

In every case, it is not just the primary use of an object that should be beautiful. All aspects should be. Picking up a pitcher gracefully is as important as pouring a libation with it gracefully.

Rehearsal can show you where the problems are and give you the chance to fix them before you stumble across them in the middle of a ritual. Rehearsal increases the ease with which a ritual is performed, adding to its beauty.

Keep all this in mind when constructing a ritual from the prayers in Part II. It is possible to create an entire ritual from these by choosing a single prayer from each of the chapters. It would be a short ritual, but complete in its way. That may even be a good way to set up a solitary ritual, perhaps for daily devotions, where brevity is a plus.

It is unlikely that a ritual like that would be satisfying for a group, however. It would probably only last about fifteen minutes, and by the time people were getting into it, it would be over.

Imagine, however, that your group is holding a ritual. In your tradition, you cast circles and as part of that you address the four directions, calling on the classical elements of Air, Fire, Water, and Earth assigned to each, using a tool connected with that element. Let's say as well that it is part of your tradition that each direction is addressed by a different person.

So there you are, sitting in a circle, and the time has come to call on the directions. The person who is to call on the first stands up and goes to the place where you've put the tools—maybe on an altar. They pick up the right tool, goes to the right direction, and pray while manipulating the tool. Then the person goes to the altar, puts the tool down, returns to their place. The next person does the same thing. You've already added several minutes to that fifteen-minute ritual.

Or maybe you're doing the purification. You pass a bowl of water around for people to purify themselves. Say everyone has to dip their fingers in the bowl, and then anoint themselves on the forehead. Then they have to pass the bowl on to the next person. Multiply this by a dozen people. Now you've *really* added time.

It's important to consider this when you're putting a ritual together. In a small group, passing a bowl may work great. But with a hundred people, some of whom have elaborate purifications they want to do? Even if each person takes only five seconds, this would stretch this part of the ritual out to nine minutes. Meanwhile, everyone is standing around waiting. Great way to kill a ritual buzz. Consider aspersing instead, perhaps accompanied by a prayer.

When you write an individual prayer, you are concerned with how the words fit together—both their meaning and their sound. You want them to express just what you want, and to be beautiful. When you are putting a ritual together, you have to treat each of these prayers as if they were words. You want the prayers to fit together in both meaning and sound; you want them to express just what you want, and you want them to be beautiful.

Remember that a ritual is a prayer writ large.

# PART II

# BUILDING RITUALS

# CHAPTER 3

# BEGINNINGS

A pure person is fit to come into the presence of the pure Holy Ones; pure objects are fit for their service; pure space is fit for them to enter. But pure of what? Of all that does not belong—mess, confusion, worries.

Would you invite honored guests to your home and not clean it first? Clean yourself spiritually; purify yourself before inviting those most honored guests, the divine beings.

The first step is to purify your sacred space; identifying it with the cosmos as seen in a sacred manner is the next. Everything you do in such a space is sacred; it is written into sacred reality. By performing actions in your microcosm, you make them real in the macrocosm.

## Openings

★ Come today to worship the Kindreds,
Come today,
always come.

★ Come we together on this holy day,
across the distances which lay between us,
to this time,
to this place,

for one strong purpose:
to worship the Holy Ones in the proper manner.

★ I call you before the Holy Ones,
into the halls of the All-Gods gathered in council.
Here we will put our petitions to them for the consideration of the Wise,
and for the granting of the True, the Right, the Just,
as those who are True, and Right, and Just decide.

★ We are here:
we were always here.
We are here now:
we were always here now.
We are here together now:
we were always here together now.
We have always been here like this:
and we are always like this again.

★ Come and make offerings:
poems or prayers, well-said,
songs or steps well-prepared.
The Deities see
The Ancestors watch
The Land Spirits look on
And they will hear you.
Come, make offerings.

★ The Gods wait well,
   those patient ones,
   and will be here when you arrive,
   ready to spend time together.

★ May the beating of the drum be the beating of your
      heart.
   When you follow the beating drum, may your heart
      follow.
   May you come whole-heartedly to the ritual.

★ A family scattered is a family still.
   Today is a family reunion in the home of our Mother
      and Father.

★ Individual in existence,
   One in purpose,
   Neither denying nor losing who each of us is,
   we are one, gathered together.

★ With hands open in giving and receiving
   we come to you confidently,
   All-Gods.

★ When the rituals are performed rightly,
   all of the ways of the soul are well:
   May this ritual be performed rightly.
   When the rituals are performed rightly,
   all of the relationships in society are well:

May this ritual be performed rightly.
When the rituals are performed rightly,
all of the state is well:
May this ritual be performed rightly.
When the rituals are performed rightly,
all of the things of Heaven and Earth are well:
May this ritual be performed rightly.
When the rituals are performed rightly,
all things that are or may be are well:
May this ritual be performed rightly.

★ We come together today as a community to worship
the Undying Ones.
This is as it should be; it is not good for people to be
alone.
When we evolved from the species that came before
us it wasn't just our larger brains that gave us an
edge,
it wasn't just the tools that our larger brains inspired
us to make that did this,
it wasn't just the upright stance that allowed us to
use those tools easily that improved our ability to
survive.
Most of all it was community.
It was our love of having other humans around us,
to help us when we were weak, to be helped when
*they* were weak,

to be protected and to protect,
to be loved by and to love,
to gather together to reassure ourselves, to know
    that things will be okay.
That is one of the great strengths of our species.
It is part of us, not decided on, but written into our
    bodies, encoded in our DNA.
We may need guidance and explanations to live well
    in communities, but we do not need outside
    information to know that we must live together
    as communities. It is who we are.
So when we come together as a community to wor-
    ship today, we are doing something that is pre-
    cisely a human thing to do.
When we worship as a community, we are worship-
    ping as fully human beings.
Let us join now in worship.

★ A school of fish, responding to currents
   A meadow of grass, responding to wind:
   each individual, each in the same pattern.
   That is us, as we come together for worship.

★ Still your fears,
   replace them with awe;
   Prepare for the Holy
   with a single mind.

★ Come to where the people are,
  Come to where the Gods are,
  Come to the drums, Come to the bells,
  Come dancing to the sacred place,
  Come dancing, Come singing, Come.

★ I call, I call, I call you here,
  to worship, to worship, the Ancient Ones.
  Listen and come to the one who calls
  who calls, who calls, who calls to you.

★ Gather by the tree that rises,
  and rise with it to celestial realms,
  where Shining Ones gather
  to hear our prayers:
  make prayers to them here.

★ Living so long in the polluted world of man
  I turn at last to the sacred land,
  the pure land of the gods,
  the holy land of the goddesses,
  which is my true home.

  *Before a tale is told:*

★ It was a long time ago—
  no one knows when, or even if (still the story is true)—
  that what happened, happened.
  It is still happening, of course, and always will—
  that's the way it is with true stories.

Listen carefully, then,
because this story is about where you come from,
or maybe were you are.
Maybe you haven't found it yet.
Maybe it is something that's already happened,
so it will explain where you are,
or maybe it's going on right now,
so it will help you decide what to do,
or maybe it hasn't happened yet—
forewarned is forearmed.
Listen carefully, then:
this story is true.

## Purifications

★   May I be pure that I might cross through the sacred.
May I cross through the sacred that I might attain
    the holy.
May I attain the holy that I might be blessed in all
    things.

★   The impure is that which doesn't fit a time, a place,
    an intent.
May this water wash the impure away,
and leave behind the fit.

★   Through pure water, I am pure.
Through pure fire, I am pure.

By the pure, I am pure
to come before the gods of incomprehensible purity.

★  I make myself pure to receive the pure as guests.

★  Everything that is not proper to my purpose today,
everything that would offend [deity name],
everything that would interfere with your worship:
May it all drain away,
removed by the purifying water,
replaced totally by that water's purity.

★  From all that I have done that I should not have
    done,
may I be purified.
From all that has come to me that should not have
    come,
may I be purified.
From all that is not in the right place.
or has happened at the wrong time,
may I be purified,
that I may put these things behind me and step
    again onto the path of the Holy Ones.
May I be pure, may I be pure, may I be pure.

★  That we aren't impure by nature, and only made
    so by error, is made clear to us in this ritual.
    Water washes away only what's on the outside,
    removes that which does not belong.

I purify you with water, then,
Making you what you truly are,
Making you what you already are,
Making you what you have always been:
pure to be in the presence of the gods.

★ May this water wash away everything that keeps me
    from seeing the sacred through which I walk, the
    Ocean of spirits through which I walk.

★ May the water with which I anoint my forehead be a
    stream to wash away the impurities of my every-
    day life.

*Ariomanus:*

★ Lion-headed god, of fiery breath,
    burn away from me all that separates myself from
        the divine.
    Fear-inspiring entity,
    do your worst,
    do your best.

## Sacred Space

★ Above and below,
    and me between.
    Around and about,
    and me in the midst.
    Before and after,
    and me here now.

★ The waters support and surround me
   The land extends about me
   The sky reaches out above me
   At the center burns a living flame.

★ Open your eyes and look around
   and see the sacred in our midst
   and see us in the midst of the sacred.

★ If you truly know that you're truly here
   then you'll truly know that the holy is here
   and always was.

★ The Sacred Space is here.
   The Sacred Time is now.
   Nowhere to travel,
   nothing to wait for.
   Just know it to be true,
   and you are there
   and you are then.

★ It is by standing here that we know this place to be
        sacred.
   It is by doing holy things that we know this day to
        be sacred.
   It is by worshiping the Holy Ones with all that we are
   that we will know that we are sacred,
   and will carry the sacred into all places,
   on all days.

★  I am here
    and I belong here.
    How could I not when every deed and decision I
        have made in my life has brought me here?
    Whether arriving here has brought me good or ill,
    or brought good or ill to others,
    here is where I belong.
    And it is from here that I must pray.

★  We have come to worship today,
    making this time sacred by worshipping
    and this space by worshipping together.

★  We are standing here.
    You are standing here.
    I am standing here.
    We are standing here.
    And today we will raise open hands
    and pray to those who are holy
    with sweet words of welcome.

★  From the home to the wild,
    I walk a sacred path.
    From the wild to the home,
    I walk a sacred path.
    The wild is sacred.
    The home is sacred.
    The wild and the home, both sacred.
    Most sacred of all, the Path between.

★   We are here.
    We are here.
    We are here.
    And here is where we will worship the Holy Ones.
    The time is now.
    The time is now.
    The time is now.
    And now is when we will worship the Holy ones.
    Never denying the holiness of Here.
    Never denying the holiness of Now.
    Never denying the presence of the Holy Ones in all
        Heres and Nows.

*In this prayer, mead is poured into a bowl, and then cast as an offering
in the directions as noted. The prayer is complemented by a closing prayer
found in chapter 11:*

★   We stand, pillars, in the center of the world,
    while all else turns about us.
    In the center, Chaos enters Cosmos.
    It endangers and enlightens it,
    gifting it with power:
    Power to the South [offering]
    Power to the West [offering]
    Power to the North [offering]
    Power to the East, [offering]
    the place of prayer, the place of light,
    the place of the Holy Ones.
    And power to the Center, [offering]

where we stand, pillars,
while all else turns about us.

★   Gods who watch over this place,
whom I don't know.
Ancestors who watch over this place,
whom I don't know.
Land Spirits who dwell in this place,
whom I don't know:
I'm leaving this offering to you, unknowing,
out of my ignorance, to the unknown.

★   East, where light rises
Are you there?
You are.
South, where light stands high
Are you there?
You are.
West, where light descends
Are you there?
You are.
North, where darkness is
Are you there?
You are.
Center, where I am
Are you there?
I am.

★ I place myself in Air, in the East I place myself,
    under the protection of Raphael I place myself.
I place myself in Fire, in the South I place myself,
    under the protection of Michael I place myself.
I place myself in Water, in the West I place myself,
    under the protection of Gabriel I place myself.
I place myself in Earth, in the North I place myself,
    under the protection of Uriel I place myself.
I place myself in the Above, in the Sky I place myself,
    under the protection of the Father I place myself.
I place myself in the Below, in the Earth I place
    myself, under the protection of the Mother I
    place myself.
I place myself in Spirit, in the Center I place myself,
    under the protection of all the Holy Ones I place
    myself.
In this moment
In this place
In the midst of the elements
In the midst of the Two
In the midst of the Center
In the midst of all the divine ones
I place myself under their protection.

★ We speak our prayers in the proper way,
to the proper directions
to those who dwell there.
Toward the East we pray,

to the spirits of thought,
the spirits of the words we use.
Toward the South we pray, to the spirits of deeds,
the spirits of our ritual acts.
Toward the West we pray,

to the spirits of emotion,
the spirits of the feelings we give.
Toward the North we pray,

to the spirits of beings,
to the spirits of the bodies that turn.
We speak in the Center,
where the directions join,
and bring us to life that we might pray:
from the Center may we always speak.

★ This space, this sacred space,
is guarded by the sacred beings of protection,
who answer those who call to them.
With confidence in their continued presence I begin
    my rites.

★ I make this sign in the East,
the sign of Air,
to the beings of Air,
to call to them, to call them here,
to come to those who worship here.
Come, you are welcome, Spirits of Air.

I make this sign in the South,
the sign of Fire,
to the beings of Fire,
to call to them, to call them here,
to come to those who worship here.
Come, you are welcome, Spirits of Fire.

I make this sign in the West,
the sign of Water,
to the beings of Water,
to call to them, to call them here,
to come to those who worship here.
Come, you are welcome, Spirits of Water.

I make this sign in the North,
the sign of Earth,
to the beings of Earth,
to call to them, to call them here,
to come to those who worship here.
Come, you are welcome, Spirits of Earth.

★ May blow from the East the wind of Air, hot and
    moist, to form its part of this circle's balance.
May blow from the South the wind of Fire, hot and
    dry, to form its part of this circle's balance.
May blow from the West the wind of Water, cold
    and moist, to form its part of this circle's balance.

May blow from the North the wind of Earth, cold
    and dry, to form its part of this circle's balance.
May the four winds join in the Center in balance.

★  That side, mundane,
   this side, divine.
   We draw the line
   for our ritual,
   for this time.

# CHAPTER 4

# THE HOME

Among the ancient Pagans, the rituals that surrounded the spirits and deities of the home and the honoring of the Ancestors were more important than the great public ones. After all, we live in our houses every day; we eat in them; we make ourselves vulnerable in sleep in them. They are our most important property, and contain most of the rest of what we own, whether simply material, like pots and pans, or sentimental, like old photographs. We need them to be safe, and to feel safe in them.

The divine beings most involved in domestic rituals are those of the border (of our land, or the door, the border between outside and inside) and those of the hearth. In other words, those of the edge and those of the center.

Hearth guardians are traditionally female; they are the soul of the enfolding home. Border guardians, on the other hand, tend to be male; they are the warriors manning the ramparts. That's how they'll be recognized in the following prayers. If you see them differently, it should be little trouble to change things around.

*Hermes:*

★ Hermes kleptōn, who protects thieves,
   instead guard my property from thieves.
   Even as you support the Cosmic Order,
   you, herald of Zeus who enforces divine law,

you, god closest to men,
enforce the little order of human law,
the way of mortals,
and the order smaller yet of this home,
my little cosmos,
 and preserve it inviolate from intruders with bur-
    glary on their minds.
Hermes, god of thieves, this time protect against
    thieves,
and send them on their way with no gain.

## The Land

*Land Spirits:*

★ Those who dwelt in this land before it was ours, and
    was still wild,
we offer you our apologies for displacing you,
with this offering of [scattered grain/corn/wheat/
    etc.; poured-out milk/beer/wine/etc.; strewn
    tobacco] we complete the cycle of gifts:
our offering for your land.
By the exchange may we be friends,
by friendship may there be peace,
and by peace may we live lives together in happiness.

*Silvanus:*

★ Silvanus of the wild,
be Silvanus of my land,
and I will pour wine to you as a libation.

*Terminus:*

★ Lord who protects borders,
  protect me, my household, my land,
  and all who enter here as guests.
  In return for which, in promise of future offerings,
  to establish, maintain, and strengthen friendship
      between us,
  this wine, this grain, this egg,
  willingly given.

## The Hearth

★ She burns in the center of the Hall of the Gods,
  and around her they gather in contemplation,
  in council.
  She makes them one family of comrades.
  When they gather where she is those who contend
      are at peace,
  those whose nature is constant motion,
  rest.
  Burner and Warmer,
  Dweller on the Hearth,
  even the gods continually praise you.
  So one would expect me to feel awe when I see
      you,
  but I feel friendship and love coming from you,
  and I can only return it in kind.

★ This fire I sit by is the Goddess of the Hearth.
   Not a sign, or a symbol, or an image, or a represen-
      tation, or a manifestation of a goddess who lives
      on some celestial, spiritual, unobserved place:
   Here in front of me is this goddess herself.
   Warmed and lit by her, and eating food cooked
      through her,
   I will sit, and know her here, and thank her for this
      wonder.

★ We gather at the fire and the fire draws us in
   and holds us in her arms.
   She speaks the words our hearts, our hearts must
      hear.
   that ever where she is, we are safe,
   safe from fear.

*Hearth Goddess, with an offering of food:*
★ We eat together, home's center,
   with the same food on our tables.
   It's nice to eat with a friend.

★ Lady who sits on the throne of the hearth,
   who appears to us in scarlet robes,
   with golden fringe:
   increase our family's peace with your welcome love.
   A stove is a hearth,
   and the goddess who watches over hearths,

watches over this stove that cooks the food of our
    family
and is the hearth of hospitality:
with the lighting of this oil lamp I bring you honor.
I bring you into my heart, a heart that loves you.

★  I place you here in the center of my house:
be the navel about which all turns;
be my home the world you support.
With your warmth enliven the house.
With your warmth enliven those who live in the
    house.
With your warmth enliven those to whom hospitality
    is given in the house.
Be, then, the very power by which hospitality is
    given,
linking those who live here with the greater
    community.
Be, then, not only the center of the house
but its connection with that which is outside the
    house.
Be the one we face and the one who faces others.
I place you here in the center of my house,
and I will worship you here.

★  See, here I stand,
with flame in my hand.

The fire is laid before me.
Everything is prepared.
The house stands about me.
Everything is prepared.
See, here I stand,
with flame in my hand.
The heart of the home
is about to be lit.
The house is about to live.
Bright Goddess,
Queen of the Hearth,
The fire which will warm us,
The fire which will cook our food,
The fire which will light our homes.
You are the Queen of the Home
and I am your priestess.
I light the heart of the home.
I awaken the house to life.

★ You are in the shining fire
here in the home's heart.
Stay with me
Stay in our home
And each day I will honor you.

★ Little fire, I will tend and feed you,
and you will bless me from your vast store.

*Brighid:*

★ A new land
A new house:
the same hearth goddess.
Welcome, Brighid;
with you on the hearth, I'm home again.

*Westyā:*

★ Your moving flames are my home's still center,
the many tongues, your tongue, speaking silence.
I will sit here and listen.
Lukipotyā [Shining Lady]

## The Door

★ Protector of the Door, be:
closed against enemies
open to friends
welcoming to guests who approach you.

★ Before opening you for the first time, Door,
let me introduce myself with this gift.
We'll be working together closely from now on,
so let's get off on the right foot.

## The Threshold

★ I'm stepping with my right foot,
over, not on you:
see my respect.

★    Rise as a wall against danger,
     lie still, a gentle pathway,
     for blessings.

## Doorposts and Thresholds

★    Upright standers,
     we walk between.
     Spirits of the doorposts,
     watch over us.
     We go out,
     We come in,
     Watch over us.

     Lying flat,
     we walk over.
     Spirit of the threshold,
     watch over us.
     We go out,
     We come in,
     Watch over us.

## The House

*Domovoi:*

★    I place this bread for you, Domovoi, next to the stove:
     may this home be prosperous,
     this family happy,
     through your help.

*Hermes:*

★ Closely have I read,
and often,
of how you stole Apollo's cattle,
and by clever stratagem sought to hide the deed
and avoid your guilt,
becoming thereby the god of thieves.
Trickster, I ask you to turn your trickery against those
  selfsame thieves,
and defeat the aims of those who would despoil this
  house.
Hermes, I praise your intelligence, which will ever
  find a way in,
and ask that it be just as effective in keeping bur-
  glars out.

*House Spirits*

★ Be under the protection of the Hearth,
House Spirits:
We will offer to you at times.

★ May the spirits of the wood and minerals that make
  up this house
live well, live honored lives.
Aware of your presence, we place ourselves under
  your protection with this offering,
and promise offerings in the future.

★   May the pillars of this home stand as erect and
        faithful as the phallus of the God.
    May its floors support it as faithfully as the wide-
        extending body of the Goddess.
    May we, those who dwell in this house,
    continually receive blessings from the presence of
        the God and Goddess.

## Ancestors

★   Ancestors,
    be present in our shrine.
    Watch over us, your children,
    giving wisdom and guidance when needed,
    and linking us together.

★   Here in this home, the Ancestors are thick about us,
    the Dead are thick about us,
    but we who live in their midst are ourselves living,
    and when we think of them, remembering them
        with a child's fondness,
    they live too, and we live together happily.

☀ CHAPTER 5

# CALLINGS

The gods aren't omnipotent. They need to know where they are wanted. They are not omniscient. They need to know which of them we want to come.

Calling the deities is good for us as well. We become aware of just what part of divine reality we wish to manifest in our midst. We can prepare ourselves for that specific being.

★ We lift our hands.
We lift our voices.
With words and gifts we offer to the gods,
calling them here.

★ Come share some time with me,
be my companion, my guest, my welcome visitor,
and I will play the gracious host to you, my friend.

★ Scary, huh, their presence?
Be brave
Hold fast
And face them proudly on your feet when they
come
And come they will
when we call.

Gathered here, with the gods all around, we have
    to ask ourselves what they want. The old stories,
    and the rituals handed down in old books, say
    clearly that they want gifts. The question is, what
    gifts? The gods and goddesses are individuals, so
    they have differing preferences. Some like liba-
    tions, some things burnt in fire. What poured
    out, what burnt, varies as well, so to please them
    we will have to learn what each most desires.
With all those differing desires, though, there is one
    thing they all want: open hands bringing gifts
    not begrudgingly, but willingly, even eagerly,
    glad to see them.
May that be what we offer them today.

★    If I have a patron deity, may I know who it is.
    If I do not, may one come and make themselves
        known to me.
    That is why I'm saying this prayer and making these
        offerings,
    as if scattering them for the winds to blow to the
        proper place,
    or casting them into the waves to follow the cur-
        rents to where they belong,
    into the ears and possession of my patron.
    My prayer is to an unknown deity,
    but is no less sincere for that.

★ With this gift, I establish hospitality with you.
  I am your host this day;
  be my host another.

★ May we sing with beauty
  that they may hear beauty
  and hearing beauty they will come:
  they will come in beauty.

★ Each one we name will hear his name,
  each one we name will hear hers.
  May each, hearing their name, come.
  We call them by their names:
  [name deities]

★ With soundless chant send your nonvoice to those
      who listen well when we are silent.

★ I sit in anticipation for those whom I have called,
  who come to those who sit and who wait.

★ When the drum beats, the gods answer.
  When they hear its call, the goddesses come.

★ May all the mysteries which surround me be known
      to me:
  I open myself up to them.

★ A door is opening, there in the air above the fire that
      is burning our offerings.

A gateway is forming, through which passes the
    road of life,
which makes its way for our world to that other,
where the gods dwell.
Look, they come; the Spirits are coming,
through the door, the gate, on the road.
Dancing, walking, beautifully moving they come,
to fill this sacred space:
everywhere you look, there are Spirits,
everywhere shining.

★   The dry sound of my rattle cries out my thirst
    I long for the presence of the Ones Who Bless.
    What I cannot say with my parched soul,
    my rattle speaks for me.
    May Those Who Hear, hear this,
    my prayer spoken in a rattle's voice,
    and may they, hearing, come to quench my thirst
        for them.

*Agni:*

★   If your tongues will speak my words
    I will feed you with butter;
    you will grow strong and carry my prayers to the
        gods.

★   Do not hide from us, in water or reed,
    fire of offering, High Priest Agni:

be strong on our altar raised to the gods,
you, first of them to receive offering.
Lap with your many tongues this butter poured
    into you,
this golden butter, clarified, pure,
into your flames, clear and pure.
Grow strong, grow high, fed by wood and butter,
increase in strength through our prayers today,
our words poured out like butter, like sweet butter,
in your praise.

*The All-Gods:*

★  Hear, All-Gods, these words of ours.
Come, all of you:
there is always room for you,
here and in our hearts.

★  My words drop into a bottomless well
and reach you,
All-Gods.

★  My words are nothing with so many given you in all
    time and space.
And so I say them,
speaking myself into that never-ending river:
All-Gods.

*Amaterasu:*

★  Come out of your cave, Amaterasu-kami,

and see the dance,
and dance yourself, before your mirror.

*Ancestors:*

★ From the first self-replicating molecule to we who
      stand here today
has been a long, precarious journey,
the bush of life branching and branching again,
with most twigs ending in brittle death, in brutal
      extinction.
Even with all its dead branches lying broken on the
      ground beneath it,
the bush still lives,
connecting our own small twig to all the rest.
We are related to all life, with many shared
      ancestors,
going back to that first self-replicating molecule,
each with their own wisdom to give us if we ask
      pleasantly.
That's why we are here on this occasion.
We have spoken sweet and kind respectful words to
      you,
the way you deserve.
Come together and join your family gathered here.

★ Ancient Ones, whose realm is the night:
We call to you, we call you here,
and when you come, may we face without fright,

the Dead, and death, from whose deep land,
we call to you, we call you here,
we call to you here, to come to us.

*Cybele:*

★  Come, Cybele, come.
Come, Cybele, come.
Come, Cybele; come Cybele,
Come, Cybele, Come.
Hear the tambourine.
Hear the sounding drum.
Hear us as we call you,
come, Cybele, come.
[repeat as desired]

*Dawn:*

★  Dawn in my heart,
Maiden who brings hope to those who despair;
light to those wrapped in darkness.

*Dionysos:*

★  Filled with ecstasy, with power, untamed,
        uncontrolled:
God of the Mad, entwined with ivy,
I open my mind to you.

★  Come roaring, with bellows of bulls,
come tearing apart, with blood-bearing hands,
Dionysos, come, with maenads in your train,
leopard-riding, come, with claws and teeth.

*Earth Mother:*

★ Broad pastured one,
who spreads beneath us,
on whom we walk,
in whom we plant,
from whom grows grass
that feeds our herds.
Mother Earth, to you we call,
to bless our rite with your holy presence.
You who give birth and receive the dead,
The beginning and the end of all.

*The God:*

★ We call upon the All-Father:
Come to us!
By the raging wind:
Come to us!
By the blaze of fire:
Come to us!
By the surging water:
Come to us!
By the cold, still earth:
Come to us!
By the Spirit of All:
Come to us!
Come to your people:
Come to us!

*The God as Death:*

★  Come, Stern Lord:
Come to us!
Out of the darkness:
Come to us!
By the tempest wind:
Come to us!
By the devouring fire:
Come to us!
By the overwhelming sea:
Come to us!
By the opening earth:
Come to us!
By the Spirit that waits:
Come to us!
Come to your people:
Come to us!

*The Goddess:*

★  We call on the Great Mother:
Come to us!
By the singing air:
Come to us!
By the dancing fire:
Come to us!
By the ocean water:
Come to us!

By the silent earth:
Come to us!
By the Spirit of All:
Come to us!
Come to your people:
Come to us!

★ When the Priestess stands in the circle,
  filled with the divine Female Power,
  she is not the symbol of the Goddess,
  she is not wearing the Goddess:
  she is the Goddess Herself,
  here among us,
  here, blessing us with what is only Hers to give.
  That is why the Priestess is standing here in this circle.
  It is why she stands in the center and waits for the
      Goddess to come.
  Let us wait with her.
  Let us sing for her.
  Let us sing for the Goddess,
  so that seeing us ready she might come.
  [singing]
  Come to us, Mother,
  Oh come to us here;
  Come to us, Goddess,
  Oh come to us here.
  [repeat as desired]

*The Goddess as Death:*

★  Come, Dark Mother,
Come to us!
Out of the night, on owl's wings:
Come to us!
By the screeching wind:
Come to us!
By the cleansing fire:
Come to us!
By the absorbing water:
Come to us!
By the resting earth:
Come to us!
By the Spirit that waits:
Come to us!
Come to your people:
Come to us!

*Hekate:*

★  You whom even Zeus reveres,
who standing at the crossroads,
where magic dwells,
watch all ways:
be at the center of my life;
may I see through your eyes.

*Iris:*

★  The rainbow is a mystery of fire in water,
sun through clouds;

since ancient times the bridge between the everyday
and the divine.
Iris, be a true herald.

*Isis:*

★ Come, Winged One, come.
Come, High Throne, come.
Come, Keening Wife, come.
Come, Loving Queen, come.
Come, Isis, come,
Come Isis, come.

*Kami:*

★ Kami of this place and this time,
I respect you, so I have come to see and praise you,
but not before I have purified myself,
becoming fit to stand in your august presence.

*Land Spirits:*

★ I see trees, I hear birds, I feel stones and dirt against
my walking feet;
insects crawl on me or buzz around me, trees stand
solid, and smaller plants bend as I push through.
The earth smells of rotting leaves, and of life.
I see and hear and feel and smell so much in this
forest.
But with my greatest attention I will miss you, Spirits, unless you make yourself known.
Come to me; if you don't want to be seen with my
eyes, come in other forms,

or even come in ways I will find hard to perceive.
I promise to wait for you with careful attention.
Only come.

★  From the branches of the trees they are peering.
From the faces of the stones they are looking.
From the surface of the waters they are rising.
They are coming here to drink this milk I have
        poured out for them.

★  On the trail of corn meal the spirits come, dancing,
their feet not smudging its golden road;
along it they come to those who have made it.

★  Come, Eagle, carrying in your feathers the Heavenly
Ones, riding to us.

*Manannán mac Lir:*

★  As I'm sitting on the sand between high tide and
        low tide,
with the cold passing almost unhindered through
        my now wet clothes,
part of me is saying, "What are you, nuts?"
But there's the other part,
the one that's reaching out eagerly,
desperately even,
wanting to see and know you,
to join hands together as friends meeting after too
        long apart.

That's the part that is taking the cold and wet and
    lighting a fire in my soul with it,
warming my freezing body.
You won't come to me unless I set out for you.
And we will meet in the middle.
That's why I'm sitting *here*, in the space between the
    land and the sea.
That's the middle, isn't it?
My prayer goes out on the ebbing tide.
May you come to meet me on the return,
riding on the crest of the waves,
crashing into my heart's shores.

★  May your horses, their manes foam-flecked,
    their hooves forever crashing onto shore,
    carry you constantly into my life,
    Manannán mac Lir, wave-rider.

★  From tearing ocean into welcoming bay,
    Come homeward, Sailor, on silver keel.
    Cross beacon-guided the shattering shoal,
    and gently come, and joyful stay.

From tearing ocean into welcoming bay,
past guardian jetty guide your boat,
and tie its rope to pillared pier,
and gently come, and joyful stay.

From tearing ocean into welcoming bay,

set foot on land with blessing touch,
and enter home, and sit at hearth.
Come homeward, Sailor; come Son of Sea:
O gently come, and joyful stay.

★ As the mist on your ocean, Mac Lir,
dissolves with the touch of the sun as it rises toward
     its height,
so may all that separates me from the presence of
     the Gods melt away.

*Nuit:*

★ You come in the silence, Nuit,
when space is left open for your infinite emptiness.
And so it is that speech, and deeds, and any search-
     ing won't find you.
Only waiting.
I sit here and wait with openness, with longing but
     no expectation.
Though all else is empty, the longing remains.
I hope you will not begrudge me that, and will still
     bring me to you.

*Selene:*

★ With your outpouring light do not just bathe my
     outside, Selene;
I offer you the hospitality of myself.
May you find a well-appointed home there.

*Soma:*

★  May he who, pressed out, is life, is power,
   May he whose roaring calls us to the ritual, to drink,
   May he, granting gifts, filling us with immortality,
   May he, King Soma, be praised in this prayer.
   May he, hearing me, come to join me in this rite.
   May my words draw him hither.

*Tree Spirits:*

★  Your skin hard and rough against mine,
   I trace with my fingers the patterns of your bark's
      folds.
   Is it your words to me?
   Do you hear *my* words to you?
   At least know the meaning of this offering.

*Unknown Deities:*

★  There are gods of all and gods of each.
   At this moment, when I don't know whom to turn to,
   gods or men,
   I know at least that there is one deity,
   or many,
   who will hear my prayer and see my need,
   and will answer me with blessings.
   Though I don't know who receives this prayer
   and this offering,
   I know you are mighty and worthy of worship.
   Accept my gifts and overlook my ignorance.

*Vāc:*

★ Each word, you.
Each syllable, you.
Each sound, you.
Each thought of utterance,
you, O Vāc.
May all my spoken words
and even all my unspoken
be you, O Vāc.

# CHAPTER 6

# PRAISE

If the gods weren't worthy of praise, they wouldn't be worthy of being gods. Like us, they like to have nice things said about them; as with our loved ones, it is a pleasure to say nice things about them. To tell their stories is a kind of praise—it tells them that you know and care about them.

★ I face east and I pray,
the Holy Ones I praise:
To the Shining Gods and Goddesses, praise.
To the Wise Ancestors, praise.
To the secretive Nature Spirits, praise.
To the Sacred Ones,
To the Holy Ones,
To the Numinous Ones:
Praise, praise, always praise.

★ I meditate on your name, chewing it over and over,
[god's name], [god's name], [god's name];
with each saying it digs deeper into me,
burrowing a path into my soul,
where it may build a home to dwell within me,
where you will live,
hearing me when I seek you out,

with no real seeking needed, you already there.
[god's name], [god's name], [god's name].

★   Words fail me in your presence
    and at your coming all that is left to me
    is wow!

*Agni:*
★   Here in this world
    There in the air
    There above the sky
    Agni burns as priest.

★   Fire is born from waters,
    who lovingly enclose him,
    feeding him like butter.

*Agni, with an offering of ghee:*
★   The shining rivers flow for Agni.
    Three streams of gold feed him.
    Fed, he bears on his back our words
    and, rising, brings them to the gods.
    First of the gods, rightly given the first,
    he carries them into the highest of heavens.

*Airyaman:*
★   If man and woman come together in marriage,
    be pleased, Airyaman.
    If those who suffer are brought to healing,
    be pleased, Airyaman.

If people live in peace,
be pleased, Airyaman.
By rightful order,
be pleased, Airyaman.

*The All-Gods:*

★ If I try, All-Gods, can I understand one of you?
No chance.
Understand two of you?
Calculations can't even begin.
Understand all of you?
A better chance, since my understanding collapses
    in the effort, and you pour into the gaps,
filling me with you, who understand yourself
    completely.
Maybe even then I can't say that I understand you,
but at least I'm where the understanding is
    going on.

★ Beyond all imagining is the glory of the gods.
Beyond all imagining is the power of the gods.
Beyond all imagining is the being of the gods.
So I stand here and imagine the best I can.

★ If, at any time in my prayers, I have omitted
    any of you,
I pour out these words,
All the gods who are.

★   Fill it as I might with statues, All-Gods,
    my shrine could never contain images of every one
        of you.
    That would take a shrine the size of a universe.
    But isn't that what this universe is?

★   I'd planned to ask you something,
    but now that you're here—

★   Holy Ones, when I try to understand you, I have to
        wonder if it is even possible; the mortal knowing
        the immortal, the small containing the large. I
        know, though, that that's not actually your wish.
        I don't think you completely understand me
        either, and want only to stand in relationship to
        me. I'll try to please you, and seek uncompre-
        hending friendship,
    All-Gods.

★   Infinite in number,
    Mind-boggling to conceive:
    Only a few of you enter my life
    and for that I am glad.
    As each comes to me I will do them honor
    as the Order impels.

    *Any or all of the gods:*
★   Words fail—
    I pray,

you come.
Words fail.
Your presence shatters them,
and pushes the pieces away,
too far from me to ever find again.
I don't care.
They have served their purpose:
they were meant to fall before you.
So small a gift for something so great.

*Aphrodite:*

★ See her, rising from the foam,
stepping onto land at the ocean's edge,
most beautiful of all that live in both,
and most beautiful than all in the land above:
Aphrodite, goddess of beauty and love.

*Apollo:*

★ When your arrows pierce my soul, Straight Shooter,
may it be only to kill any falsehoods there.
Your music is true, Apollo.

*Cernunnos:*

★ He's laughing at me.
No sound escapes from his mouth,
his eyes don't dance,
and his body is still
(so still).
But have no doubt—

he is laughing.
I'm sorry I'm not as perfect as you, Cernunnos,
moving without action or changing,
being, in fact, the fate that allows or denies all
     change.
But I promise I'll sit with you,
until someday we will laugh together.
Although still at me.

*Ceres:*

★ With one hand she blesses, with the other she
     proffers grain,
feeding spirit and body of those who pray to her,
Need-provider, Ceres the Grower.

*Earth:*

★ I will stand only a moment before my shrine to bow
to your image,
and then I will go outside and place my hands on
     your very self,
a loving caress.

★ Each step a child's caress.

*Energy Spirits:*

★ Each sun ray,
Each water drop,
Each gust of wind,
Each colliding atom,

Each spirit that formed coal, or oil, or gas:
Each keystroke is a hymn to you.

★ A friend who is filled    with the force of life.
   A god who is great    with the sweetest grace.
   A lord who is laughing    with the might of love.
   A Healer is Freyr    who makes things whole.
   And he is the one    with wonderful gifts
   holding my health    with a hand that is strong.

*The God:*

★ Lord of the Shining Sky
   who sees all we do.
   We praise you.
   We sing to you.
   We offer to you.
   The one who stands high
   is worthy of praise.
   The one who stands straight
   is worthy of praise.
   The one who stands stiffly
   is worthy of praise.
   Mystic Phallus, the Moving One
   Mystic Phallus, the Shining One
   Mystic Phallus, the Shattering One
   Who opens all doors
   Who breaks all locks.

*The God and Goddess:*

★ When God and Goddess unite in love,
mystery is born,
and from mystery all things.
Mystery born from mystery born from mystery.
The Great Mystery:
this is their gift.

*The Goddess:*

★ She is great and not to be held
because it is her arms that hold.
She is ever-present and not to be seen
because there is nothing to compare her to.
Ride across the plains
and you are on her body.
Climb the mountains
and you climb her breasts.
Go into the ocean
and you are in her very womb.
Mystic Yoni, not to be held.
Mystic Yoni, not to be seen.
Mystic Yoni, only to be loved.
Mystic Yoni, Gift-Giver.
Mystic Yoni, Birth-Giver.

★ I can't really forget you because my life is your living.
If I seem to not remember,
know that that's just my mind and not my heart.

★ Your are She, the One without beginning.
  You are the Mother of All, Who gives birth to the
      world.
  You are the Essence, from Whom all things are
      formed:
  Wherever we may look, You will be there.
  Your are She of many names:
  When Your true face is known, all naming ceases.
  In Your presence all stop in wonder:
  All life is a prayer to You.

★ Are you not in this day, in the light and the dark?
  Are you not in this month, in the growing and the
      decrease?
  Are you not in this year, in the warmth and the cold?
  Are you not in all these things you have given birth?
  Are you not in all your children, one of whom stands
      here speaking words of praise?

★ Too much everything,
  too much owned and done,
  too much required of me, owed by me,
  has driven me to the presence of the Goddess,
  where there is never too much.

  *Gʷouwindā:*
★ Your outstretched enfolding arms offer cattle,
  pour out rich milk,

that we might, like children, grow in prosperity.
Leading cows you come to your worshippers,
who, pouring golden butter, come to you.

*Herne:*

★ Herne, your antlers fill the sky,
shading out the stars that shine there,
bringing in the darkness your own kind of light,
the light of mysteries, the light that only you can
    bring,
in your night.

*Inanna:*

★ It is she, Inanna
she is the great Inanna.
The victor over enemies in war,
It is she, Inanna;
she is the great Inanna.
The victor over barriers to love,
It is she, Inanna;
she is the great Inanna.
The victor over all that opposes us,
It is she, Inanna;
she is the great Inanna.

*Indra:*

★ With a cast of the vajra you killed the serpent Vṛtra
and the waters erupted, lowing with pleasure.
The six-eyed armless one lay prostrate after you did
    this, O Indra.

A soma draught intoxicates you,
you burn with divine flame when you ride forth, O
    Indra,
when you ride against demons,
and all your enemies tremble.

*Isis:*

★ Mother, Wife, Mourner, Magician;
Sistrum-Rattler, Revenge-Director,
Ecstasy-Inducer, Love-Inspirer:
Isis.

*Lugh:*

★ You came to the court which feasted at Tara,
and, challenged, listed your skills:
Champion and harper, and doctor,
cupbearer and scribe and poet;
on and on the list went; each time came the answer,
"We have one of those, you cannot enter."
Then came your punch line:
"Do you have anyone who can do all these things?"
They did not, of course, and had to let you enter.
You became the true king, saved the goddess's chil-
    dren from inhospitable oppressors.
Shining-speared champion,
I have told this tale of yours, and will tell more at
    other times.

*Manannán mac Lir:*

★ Who is it whom we see?
   We see a man with silver hair, with silver beard,
        flecked with salt foam.
   We see a man in a cloak of no colors, or is it of every
        color?
   When it moves, it hides and reveals; sometimes
        things show through it,
   sometimes they ripple as if on their surface,
   sometimes they fade softly at their edges, as if
        imprinted on fog.
   We see a man holding an apple branch:
   its fruit is golden, and rings like bells when he
        shakes it.
   And its golden-toned music soothes us, would sing
        us to sleep if we listened to it for long.
   But he shakes the branch and the apples sound just
        until we hear it,
   and leaves an ache in our hearts when its echoes fade.
   We see a man who drives a chariot without reins.
   His horses ride sure-footed, wave-maned across
        the sea,
   which seems a flowered plain beneath the turning,
        diamond-flashing wheels.
   We see a man who is alternately too bright for our
        eyes to bear,

and then compassionate in his gaze.
We see this man. Whom is it we see?
That's easy—we see Manannán, a guide to those on
    journeys,
who shows the way where there are no tracks;
We see a comforter who smooths away memories
    that rot the heart.
We see Manannán mac Lir,
Comforter and Guide,
Son of the Sea.

*Menot:*

★ Measuring and measuring again,
checking your math over and over,
your reckoning always right,
but you faithfully measuring out the next.
When I doubt,
and hesitate,
and check my calculations for precision,
I am worshipping you, who expect no more from me
and no less.

★ Straight
True
Right
Well-formed and measured.
Clear
Pure
are you, Menot.

*Mercury:*

★  Clever Mercurius:
   God of commerce, god of prosperity,
   God of wisdom, god of travel,
   Guide of souls:
   I offer you my worship.

*The Mississippi River:*

★  This small stream, that river, are your children,
         Father of the Waters.
   But they feed into you,
   so who is father of whom?
   Where do you come from,
   where is your fatherhood,
   if you come from them?
   This is what I think:
   Each of these streams, rivers,
   each rain drop that falls on this land,
   has a spirit,
   and each spirit joins in you,
   so that you, whose source is them,
   all together,
   connect them like a founding ancestor his
         descendents,
   them your children,
   and you, Mississippi, their father.

*Moon:*

★ It's sweet to rest in the night under the moon,
a queen surrounded by her handmaiden stars,
who empties her store of love over my head,
white light, silver light, warm light:
this is her gift to me and to all who look toward her.
You are in the sky above me, and you are in my heart.

*Night:*

★ Exactly how many eyes do you have, Night?
I keep counting them,
and each time I come up with a different number.
However many there are,
when they look down may they find me acting
    virtuously.
Or if they don't, I hope that, seeing what *other*
    people do,
you'll understand.
I lose myself in the wonder of your infinite blackness,
And pierced by the light of your unnumbered stars,
rest in the confidence of your mercy.

*Ocean Spirits:*

★ Each drop of wind-blown salt spray is a spirit of the
    ocean, among whom I pray, and to whom I pray.

*Oghma:*

★ If I wanted to do something really stupid,
would you stop me, Oghma?

Of course not;
your job is to advise and inspire, not control.
Thanks.

*Pan:*

★    Io Pan, the shout in the hills,
Io Pan, the hooves on the rocks,
Io Pan, the song in the wild:
Io Pan, Io Pan.
Io Pan, the scattering of the flocks,
Io Pan, the singing of the pipes,
Io Pan, the roaring in the fields:
Io Pan, Io Pan.
Io Pan, the goat,
Io Pan, the man,
Io Pan, the god:
Io Pan, Io Pan.

★    Great Pan, you have not died,
but live always among those who call you,
with prayers, with songs,
with dance and the beaten drum,
we call you,
we worship you,
we celebrate you,
Great Pan, undying.

*Pele:*

★   An old woman or a young one,
      but whenever I see you, you burning as flowing
         magma.
      Hair's tresses which when cool and hard, still burn
         inside,
      forming these islands,
      are yours, Pele, clearly so.
      Whether I see you sitting on the edge of the road,
      or in my room,
      or even just in my imagination,
      I will give you leis,
      which aren't as beautiful as you.

*Perkʷúnos:*

★   My voice might not be as loud as yours,
      but it comes from my essential being too.
      May it rise through the crash of clouds and into your
         ears, Perkʷúnos,
      you who obliterate all that stands in your way.
      May I be filled with the booming brightness you hurl
         and not by my fears.
      May my body tremble with the strength of your
         arms and not my weaknesses.
      May all I do be with your unfailing accuracy and
         your power which cannot be withstood.

*Perun:*

★ The arrows of Perun drive enemies away,
and enforce justice, and grant fertility.
God with flaming hair, with burning face,
I watch you come with the clouds
to perform your mighty deeds.

*Poseidon:*

★ Blue-maned Earth-shaker,
Lord of Horses, whose realm is the sea:
I stand on your shore and watch your waves as they
    roll in and out,
each one singing a song of praise to you,
and I join in with my prayer.

*River Spirits:*

★ Crossed by a bridge, your waters are still as sacred as
when our ancestors slogged across them at fords.
Perhaps *more* sacred, since they are undefiled by our
    muddy stirrings.
Although held aloft, I am still connected,
and still honor you, River Spirit.

*Rock Spirits:*

★ Hey, I recognize you, rock.
Do you know *me*?
I'm the one who says "Hi" to you when I see you.
We can be good friends, you and me.
I'll say "Hi" next time I see you.

*Silvanus:*

★  Silvanus of the woods
   is Silvanus of the fields,
   protecting each one constantly,
   guarding all our lands faithfully.

*Spirits of Places or Things:*

★  This is small, but it has its spirit, which I honor.

*Star Goddess:*

★  I didn't think it was possible to fall up.
   But I find myself falling into your body,
   Queen of the Stars.

*Storm God:*

★  After the destruction of your thunderbolt, the rains
   come and the fields grow green.
   Too often I pray for your demolition of obstacles,
   and too rarely for a good to replace them.
   Even as I pray to you for your raw power,
   use it to remove as well this weakness of mine which
      separates:
   the end from the beginning,
   destruction from creation,
   your fire from the life-giving water that cools and
      feeds the earth as you pass by.

★  With a right arm with strength enough to cleave
      universes,
   he slew the serpent who thought he could destroy
      the cosmos.

And every day with steadfast dedication to the right
    cause
he renews the battle against disorder with his aim
    never swerving from true.
Axe-Wielder and Bright-Striker:
did you hear me telling your story?

★  We speak to the Lord of the Lightning,
we seek out the Lord of the Right,
to Him, the ever-bright Champion,
a hymn to banish the night.

For when he comes,
he comes in the darkness.
And when he comes,
he brings in the light.

A flash that cuts through the grayness,
a crash that deafens our ears,
a spike that pins down the Chaos,
a strike that softens our fears.

For when he comes,
he comes in the darkness.
And when he comes,
he brings in the light.
With rain, he brings us the greening,
with grain, he brightens our days,

with might, he drives away falseness,
with right, he opens our ways.

For when he comes,
he comes in the darkness.
And when he comes,
he brings in the light.

For truth, he slays all confusion,
for youth, he stands as a star,
the day, he shows in the storm cloud,
the way, he marks from afar.

And when he comes,
he comes in the darkness.
And when he comes,
he brings in the light.

*Sun:*

★   If I look too long with unshielded eyes,
they, cut right through by your penetrating spears,
will burn into blindness, will bring me to dark,
a fate undesired by me, and by *you.*
Your pride in your might deserves to be known,
which never with unseeing eyes would it be.
Even not looking, then, is worship of you.
Know this, then: averting my eyes, I still praise;
I honor with words, though perhaps not my gaze.

★   Now in the sky is the highest flying of eagles
He with the eye looks down on us.

See, there he is,
Giver of light.
See, there he is,
Giver of warmth.
Who can hide from his bright spear?
Who can hide from his sharp arrows?
They find prey.
They find predator.
They find both eater and eaten.
He sees the one who walks on the road;
May it be his road we walk on.

★ Bright One
Blazing One
Flaming One
Shining One
Burning One
Hot One
Revealer of Truth
Shower of the Road
Nothing is seen without your light
but you cannot be seen.
Truth burns our eyes.
We are not strong enough to see it.
We walk it instead.
The straight road leads to you.

★  The eagle of the Sun rises high
    with the burning ball in his claws.
    He can see us here.
    No one can hide.
    When the Sun is high
    dishonesty hides away.
    No evil can stand the great light.
    Secrets are done by the moon
    but the Sun makes everything clear.

★  Shine your rays, your beams, your light,
    on all who need your light, your warmth, your
        presence.
    All that lives requires your brightness,
    and all that speaks owe you their praises:
    Sun, who looks on the world below, I honor you
        today.

★  The earth turns its circles with you as its midpoint,
    you are at the center of our system of planets,
        moons, asteroids, comets;
    your well of gravity holds each in its moving place:
    you are the one who gives order to your
        dependents.
    You do all these things, for you are great, Earth's star.
    Whether god or nuclear furnace, you deserve these
        words of praise.

*Thor:*

★ With ruddy beard and unwithstandable crashing
      hammer, you wage unceasing battle against
      giants and serpents,
all of whom fall before you, Thor; even the greatest
      snake of all,
the World-Encircling Serpent, your oldest enemy,
will know your hammer bringing it to death
      in the end.
Yet such immense and divine power,
which someone like you could easily wield against
      anyone according to your whim,
which streams in you as if it were blood, suffusing
      every cell of your divine body,
urging you on to battle,
that most, gods and men, giants and dwarves,
would be unable to rein in;
you can control it, Thunderer.
You take the side of the common folk against every-
      one who tries to oppress them.
How easy it would be for you to be an oppressor
      yourself, Thor!
But your brusque facade hides a noble heart,
and so you know *true* nobility when you see it,
nobility, not of blood, but of deeds and honor.
For fighting on the side of true order I praise Thor!

*Vayū:*

★ The wind that blows whistles between branches,
the wind that pours over plains,
the wind that rips between city towers:
this is Vayū, who brings the words of the gods,
bearing them on his back,
truth's steed, Ṛta's horse,
who brings omens and knowledge,
who brings sacred wisdom
to those who stand in it and speak prayerful words
for it to blow away.

*Viṣṇu:*

★ With one step he measured out the earth:
He is Viṣṇu, great in creation.
With one step he measured out the air:
He is Viṣṇu, great in creation.
With one step he measured out the sky:
He is Viṣṇu, great in creation.
With three steps he measured out the three worlds:
He is Viṣṇu, great in creation.

*Water Spirits:*

★ If I could slide between the raindrops, why would
    I want to?
Why avoid the purifying water that runs over me,
    carrying untruth away?
Do you know, water spirits, that you do this?

Not just feeding the earth but supporting truth?
I wouldn't avoid truth, so I don't avoid *you*.

*Xák<sup>w</sup>öm Népöt:*

★ Unkindled water,
hot blood flowing,
twin horses, shining:
he rides within.

# CHAPTER 7

# THANKSGIVINGS AND GRACES

It's very rude to ask for something and then not thank the person who gives it to you. Divine beings are people too, even if not human, and they like to be thanked. People who always give and are never thanked tend to stop giving. Something to remember.

The food and drink we consume become actual parts of our bodies. Besides being a polite thing to do, a grace blesses them, which means that we consume the sacred, which means that we become *made up* of the sacred.

## Thanksgivings

★ Even if "Thank you" would be enough, I offer you
    this in gratitude for answering my prayer.

★ If I have forgotten your presence today, [god's
    name],
   thinking I faced troubles all alone,
   forgive me this failing.
   Knowing that now, when I had the time to stop and
    think,
   I knew that you were there
   and that your help made things easier,
   made adversities gentler,

slowed my anger
cleared my thinking,
so that my judgments came, as much as is possible,
from a peaceful heart.
We can take if for certain, can't we, that your help
    will be needed again tomorrow?
When I need your help then,
if I don't think of you then,
in the heat of the moment,
please don't hold it against me.
When time comes for reflection I will think of you
    again with thanks.

*Cars:*

★ Though you can't really say it's alive,
my car drinks the blood of plants and animals that
    died long ago.
So I thank their spirits for making it possible for me
    to drive to where I will buy my own food,
whose spirits I will also thank.

*The God and Goddess:*

★ From those into whose hands we place a gift we
    expect words of thanks,
from those to whom we mail one, a thank-you note.
Those who don't follow these rules of etiquette we
    call rude.
We don't want you to call us rude, Mother and
    Father,

or to be rude even if you are too polite even to
    think it,
so we thank you for your many presents,
especially the ones you're giving us now.

*Sequana: (Goddess of the river Seine, who has been represented riding in a
boat, which is identified with the Isle de la Cité.)*

★ Far from where the river springs,
the ship parts the unstopped river,
at the heart of a city brightly lit,
renowned for art; for beauty and splendor;
your gift to the world, Sequana,
and for this my gift to you.

*Taranis:*

★ Praise to you, Taranis, riding in your wagon from
    beyond the mountains,
its wheels spraying rain with each turn,
over the waiting, parched land.
Such a gift inspires one in return.
Ours is so little compared to yours, but it's our best,
    Thunderer,
and given in true gratitude.

## Graces

★ Gathered here with family and friends, we take
    time to consciously think of everything the Gods
    deserve to be thanked for. In fact, even if they
    had done nothing in this last year but gather us

to be here with our loved ones, they would be
deserving of gratitude. For this, and for so much
else, thank you, Holy Ones, who respond to
our love and gifts with those of your own. Your
people here today will always thank you, with
sincerity, with mindfulness, with daily and true
devotion, for all you give us.

★ Blessings and thanks to the earth from which this
food comes.
Blessings and thanks to the plants and animals from
which it is formed.
Blessings and thanks to the people who brought it
forth and prepared it for us today.
And blessings and thanks to that One,
Infinite, Mysterious,
lying behind it all and giving it and us our being.

★ This drink, life's changing.
This food, life's form.

★ Seated across from us,
or to our right or left,
or in their own mysterious sacred say,
may the Gods come to eat with us.

*Animal Spirits:*
★ Grown, gathered, and ground, this grain is Earth's gift.
Bred, born, and butchered, this beef is Earth's blood.

We who eat do not forget.
Our eating is worship of those whose gift and blood
   this is.

*The God:*

★ The grain was thrust into the ground:
   it became a baby.
   It grew into a plant:
   it became a child.
   It produced seed:
   it became a man.
   It was cut down:
   it became our bread.
   Fertile God, who freely cast the gloried seed in the
      welcoming body of Earth,
   we worship you when we eat this bread.

★ Mixing, joining together.
   Slapping against the board, kicking in the womb.
   Kneading, moving down the birth canal.
   Rising, coming into the world.
   Baking, passing through the flames.
   Eating: he is in us.

★ The God goes into the grain: the God *is* the grain.
   He grows as the grain grows, for he is the grain.
   He is cut down, he is threshed, with the grain,
   the God who is the grain.
   He is ground into flour, which is the God.

Baked from the flour formed from the grain,
the bread both contains and is the God:
by eating it we draw the God in,
by consuming it the God becomes part of our bodies.
We re-form the threshed and ground God.

*The God and Goddess:*

★ Though my food may be fast,
may my life be long:
this is my prayer,
God and Goddess.

*Spirits of Food:*

★ Praise to you, souls of the plants and animals whose
lives were spent to make this food:
May these words turn your deaths into a holy sacrifice.

*Vedic Gods:*

★ You are fire in water, Agni, in the lightning-filled rain.
You are fire in water, Soma, in the inspiring plant.
You are fire in water, Apam Napat, in the gold palace.
Fire in water is the source of greatest power
and fire in water is what I drink here.

*Water Spirits:*

★ Praise to all the spirits, the gods and goddesses, of
all the rivers of the world.
This drink is of their waters, filling me with them.
Praise and thanks.

CHAPTER 8

# CONSECRATIONS AND BLESSINGS

Most prayers seek either to put us into a relationship with the divine, to ask for something from the divine, or both. Consecrations and blessings are perhaps the purest forms of these.

Both put something (or someone) into the keeping of a deity. The difference is that a consecration transfers *to* the divine, while a blessing asks for a transfer *from* the divine. Consecration is a gift *to* the divine, while blessing asks for a gift *from* the divine.

## Consecrations

★ I separate you from mundane use by these words
   spoken in the presence of the holy;
   I dedicate you to its service.

★ Sacred and holy be this [tool] of mine,
   through it, may I know the blesséd and the divine,
   by ancient laws and by new design,
   my gods invoke, my space define.

★ This tool will be used in the service of the Holy Ones,
   so may it be made holy by them through this
   prayer,

may it be suitable to the purpose to which I will put it,
to the sacred service it will perform.

★  May this cloak be consecrated to the Mighty Ones,
that covered by it I might be covered by them,
wrapped in their protecting embrace.

★  May this tool be infused with a bit of their power,
the Goddess, the God,
that through it I might perform great deeds in their
     names.

★  May this knife be all knives, so all that I cut with it
     might be cut in all the worlds.

*A deity or deities:*

★  When I bless this [tool], may it be with the power of
     [name of deity/deities].
When I hold it, may it be [him/her/them] holding it.
When I use it, may it be with [his/her/their] power.
May it be [his/hers/theirs].
May it be mine.

*The Elements: (First purify the tool. With the mention of each element,
touch the tool with an appropriate tool or symbol.)*

★  Air, look at this carefully.
Remember it so that you'll recognize it again next
     time you see it,
next time you run across it in your sphere of
     influence

or if you have yourself wandered out of it.
You're responsible now.
If the past is a guide, I know you won't fail.

Fire, look at this carefully.
Remember it so that you'll recognize it again next
    time you see it,
next time you run across it in your sphere of
    influence
or if you have yourself wandered out of it.
You're responsible now.
If the past is a guide, I know you won't fail.

Water, look at this carefully.
Remember it so that you'll recognize it again next
    time you see it,
next time you run across it in your sphere of
    influence
or if you have yourself wandered out of it.
You're responsible now.
If the past is a guide, I know you won't fail.

Earth, look at this carefully.
Remember it so that you'll recognize it again next
    time you see it,
next time you run across it in your sphere of
    influence
or if you have yourself wandered out of it.

You're responsible now.
If the past is a guide, I know you won't fail.

★  Air, I place you on one side, where you can bless
        and protect this [tool].
   Fire, I place you on one side, where you can bless
        and protect this [tool].
   Water, I place you on one side, where you can bless
        and protect this [tool].
   Earth, I place you on one side, where you can bless
        and protect this [tool].
   Spirit, I place you around and in the center,
   all through, where you can bless and protect this
        [tool],
   as if it were yourself.

★  With all impurities removed,
   may this [tool] be filled with the sacred power
   of Air,
   of Fire,
   of Water,
   of Earth,
   and with the spirit that joins and enlivens them.

★  [Hold object] I bless you.
   [Lift the object up and then back down] Air
   [Rub the object until there is a feeling of warmth]
        Fire

[Softly stroke the object in a clockwise inward spiral]
    Water
[Hit object with an open palm, not allowing it to
    bounce back] Earth
[Hold object in cupped hands and blow on it] Spirit
You are blessed with words and actions.

## Blessings

★   With each drop of water,
    with this consecrated water,
    receive the blessings of the Holy Ones.

★   With the touch of this flower,
    this beauty of the earth, this glory of nature,
    be filled with beauty, be filled with glory,
    be filled with the blessings of the earth, of nature,
    be filled and blessed by that which surrounds us.

★   May this [object] that I put around your neck be a
        sign of the protection and concern of [god's
        name], and as a constant reminder to you and to
        others of [his/her/their] ever-watchful presence.

*The Elements:*

★   Not a whirlwind, but a cooling breeze.
    Not an inferno, but a cheerful hearth.
    Not a flood, but a quenching draught.
    Not an avalanche, but a ground on which to stand.

No dangers from the elements, but blessings:
may my words bring this gift to you.

★   By Air be blessed, be blessed by the four.
By Fire be blessed, be blessed by the four.
By Water be blessed, be blessed by the four.
By Earth be blessed, be blessed by the four.
By Spirit be blessed, be blessed by the five.
By the four and the five be blessed.

*The God and Goddess, for a child:*

★   Just for a moment, it's not your father standing here,
   but the God.
Just for a moment, it's not your mother standing
   here, but the Goddess.
From past days,
through this day,
to all days:
they are here,
and they are blessing you with all they possess.
For all your life, it is your father standing here.
For all your life, it is your mother standing here.
From past days,
through this day,
to all days:
we are here,
and we are blessing you with all we possess.

★    Look, overarching sky, under whose gaze we pass
        our days,
    see this person I bring before you:
    bless them!
    Look, long-extending earth, upon whose breast we
        live our lives,
    see this person I bring before you:
    bless them!
    Look, see, bless, Sky and Earth!

    *The Goddess:*

★    Be blessed, be blessed, be truly blessed,
    by these triple words,
    by this triple touch,
    by this triple prayer,
    be blessed by the Goddess,
    by growth, by fullness, by the dark,
    by Maiden and Mother and Crone,
    be blessed, be blessed, be three times blessed,
    by the threefold Goddess be blessed.

# CHAPTER 9

# TIMES OF THE DAY

Of all the degrees of time, it is the day that affects us the most strongly. We get up, we get ready for the day, we go to work, we come home, we get ready for bed, we go to sleep. We watch the sun rise higher in the sky, and feel the warmth and light grow. We watch the sun set in a blazing sky, and feel the dark and chill descend. We see the stars appear and paint the dark with their light, and then comes the dawn. The sun returns, and the cycle begins again.

When we observe these moments with sacred words, we sanctify them (or we recognize their already-existing sacredness, which is essentially the same thing). The most mundane act becomes sacred. We are put in touch with the sacred each moment. We live sacred days.

## False Dawn

★ False dawn after darkness is comforting.
   But soon—
   Oh, the glory!

## Dawn

★ Your singing brings the sun, which I need,
   but in it I hear that this day you're announcing
      means one less in my life.

Your morning song is my mourning song.
Even though you herald the sun, I find it hard to feel
   affection toward you,
but a goddess who can bring both light and death
   deserves honor.
Take this prayer as such.

★  On my left and right stand pillars,
   those between which the Sun makes his entrance.
   And I, like Dawn, invite and welcome Him into this
      day.

★  When you climb heaven's vault,
   your hands beyond counting stretch out to all living
      things,
   gently shaking them all awake.
   "Arise!" you say, "Day is here!"
   and rising we lift our hands to yours:
   you who are One, shining.

★  Do not delay, Dawn, to rise from your rosy bed,
   to speak the words the Sun wishes spread:
   that you come, that he comes behind,
   scattering before the sorrows dark has spread:
   Do not delay, Dawn, do not delay.

★  The young maiden Dawn is the bringer of comfort,
   deserving of praise.
   To you, lovely one, these words.

★  Dawn rises in the East
   She pulls her cloak behind her
   It covers the sky while she pushes away night.
   Slowly grows in the East the golden flower
   Slowly its bud opens
   and then, suddenly, surprisingly,
   with a flash of golden light,
   He is there.
   The sun is born again.
   She has raised him again
   He is freed from the earth.
   He spreads his wings
   and climbs into the sky.
   His eye looks down
   and we look up.
   People awake
   Cattle awake
   Singing birds awake.
   Creatures of the night go to sleep
   Secrets hide
   Deeds are done in the open.
   Day begins.

★  When the sky is red with the
   light of the morning,
   I lift my hands in a cup to catch your gifts.
   That is when the young dancer

goes through the sky
and covers it with her cloak.
The morning is a good time,
a time to think of the day to come.
I stand on the grass
wet with your tears
and think of you.

★   I awake with the Sun's light
and dance forth with Dawn.

★   Sing into being over the horizon,
the rose, the many pinks of your coming,
and waken our minds from their dream-bestowed
    haze.
Open our eyes, ready our ears,
for the thundering flash,
for the sudden shout,
with which the sun will bound over the horizon
through the gates opened by you,
who are welcome to my night-darkened soul.

★   Dawn, I have seen you come and been happy before:
receive this offering.
Sun, I have seen you come and been happy before:
receive this offering.
Night, I have seen you come and been happy before:
receive this offering from one who holds you in high
    esteem.

I will see you again, and see your daughters the stars.
Now is the time to turn toward your sisters, Dawn
    and the Sun,
welcoming them with this well-intentioned offering.

★  On the sky's dew rainbow
    come swiftly, softly, into my heart, rosy maiden,
    veiled in pinks,
    Dawn.

*Aushrine:*

★  Riding the rainbow, rise in the East,
    singing Aushrine,
    singing, shining.

*Uṣas:*

★  Receiving the infant, shining in your lap,
    from the hands of your dark sister,
    send it on its way to look down on those who wor-
      ship well,
    on those whose steps it guides by Ṛta.

## Morning

★  I accept the gift of this day
    and will make it one to be proud of.

★  I am born again this morning with this morning's
    birth.

*The All-Gods:*

★ All-Gods, I thank you for guiding my soul and the
     world through the darkness into light,
  and I pray to you, and most of all to [god's name],
     to whom I am especially devoted,
  that you be with me today, with blessings and
     protection.

★ This day, this morning,
  I pray to the Old Gods, the gods of my people,
  you have given me blessings on so many days past:
  grant them to me today.
  May I, a faithful worshipper,
  flourish in happiness in your concern.

★ "Was it for this I was born?"
  asked Marcus Aurelius
  "For lying in bed in the morning?"
  Wake me, move me, get me up,
  Gods and Goddesses, Holy Ones,
  to go about my proper work,
  that which I am meant to do.

★ Waking in the morning, I think of you,
  of you, All-Gods,
  of whom my last thought was last night
  and toward whom my thoughts will turn,
  again and again,
  as I live this day.

★ This day, this morning,
   I pray to the Old Gods,
   the gods of my people.
   You have given blessings on so many days past:
   grant them to me today.
   May I, a faithful worshipper,
   flourish in happiness in your concern.

★ All the Kindreds, I ask of you this day:
   May I live a life of Quality.
   May I think artful thoughts.
   May I speak artful words.
   May I perform artful deeds.
   May I live a good life under your guidance.

★ Each action today yours, Striker.
   Each thought today yours, Measurer.
   Each decision today on what is right yours, Shining
       Sky Father.
   Each moment yours, All-Gods, today.

*Ancestors:*

★ Yesterday has gone to the Ancestors.
   Today is a new life.
   From the Ancestors I ask the continuing wisdom of
       yesterday
   and from the Gods continuing guidance for today.

*Sun:*

★ Maybe I'm awake after a poor night of too little
   sleep and disturbed dreams,

but as the saying goes, "I may have risen, but I
   refuse to shine."
Sun, you have risen, and as always you shine:
and *such* shining!
Spare some shining for *me*,
your heat my blood's warmth,
gently but forcefully get and keep me moving.
If I can stay alert until noon, I can make it through
   the rest of the day,
and I'll think of you when you are highest, most
   powerful, and shining with your greatest beauty,
and pray to you with shining words.

★   I see, Father Sun, in the skylight above,
   the blue you have brought.
   And, although I have not yet seen you yourself,
   I praise your necessary presence.

★   New sun, newly seen, bring new things into my life;
   bring joyous things,
   bring love, and life, and laughter.

★   This day is one less I have to live.
   May I see it instead as a gift,
   Goddess of morning.

## Noon

★   High noon and a short pause,
   and a short gaze at you,

and then a return to my day
as you go on with yours.

★ They say that dawn is a goddess.
They say that the coming of night is a goddess.
I say that noon is a god,
whose disk blesses and shields.
You whose might is irresistible,
unable to be overcome,
look kindly on me, your worshipper.

*Earth:*

★ By your slow turning you have brought me to this
        moment when I can feel the power of the sun,
the power of a Lord at his zenith,
a power which warms me and lights my way.
Mother Earth, this is therefore a moment to praise
        not just Him—
and I do, indeed, praise Him for all his splendor—
but to praise you as well, for giving me this time
        when he might shine so brightly.

*Sun:*

★ You, rising in the morning, in all that glory,
seem in my memory to have been a small thing
        beside you,
shining, have risen to your *greatest* glory,
to your greatest height above our land,
there in the South.

Fill the hands that, empty cups, reach for you with
    some small part of that glory,
small enough for a human being to handle.
I bring my light-encrusted hands in toward my heart,
where they overflow, filling me with those captured
    rays of yours,
filling me with the life that your invincible searing,
    which none can resist,
gives to living things.

★ Glory; Glory and unimaginable power,
generated by the joining together of the very build-
    ing blocks of the universe,
creating the very building blocks of the universe,
radiating in all directions,
until a fraction of it falls on my upturned eyes.
And even this tiny piece of all you produce is beyond
    what my eyes can stand:
I see you through a closed-lid curtain.
May you grant me all the insight I can stand;
not just in the world you so obviously light,
but even in my submerged soul:
illuminate my darkest secrets,
Sun, Lord of Noon.

## Sunset

★   As night slides in softly, softly, over the resting land,
like sunset's rooster I sing the praises of the All-Gods,
and of the sun whose absence will end in dawn.

★   The young maiden Dusk is the bringer of sweet rest,
deserving of praise.
To you, lovely one, these words.

★   With the darkening of the world would come a
darkening of my soul,
a shadow on my heart, my self,
if I did not know you would be with me, Mother
Moon,
or if not you,
then your children the stars, their unnumbered eyes
keeping watch over me in the black of night.

★   I look west and fall into the fading light that brings
rest to my soul.
Calm, peace, sleep: bring these,
Goddess of the growing night,
God of the dimming light.

★   Good night, Sun, as you go to sleep;
I will soon enough sleep myself.
We will both wake in the morning and share another
day together.

# Before Sleep

★  Gods of dreams, goddesses of visions,
    guide me on this journey.

*The Goddess:*

★  Mother of the World's children,
    rock me to sleep
    and watch my dreams.

★  Mother, with your calming hands, smooth away
        the worry lines this day has etched on my face,
        my heart, soothing me into restoring sleep.

*Manannán mac Lir:*

★  The slow lapping of soft waves on the sand lulling me,
    your horses carrying me into dreams
    where I awake within a world more real.

*Morpheus:*

★  Protect me while I sleep, Morpheus,
    keep my body safe,
    bring dreams that teach,
    bring dreams that heal,
    bring dreams of comfort and peace,
    a peace only a god can give.

# Night

★  It seems as if the whole world is asleep.
    Although I know that isn't true,

Gods of the night, whose worship I keep,
may I join with those who do.

★ In the stillness of night, I free myself from the
business of the day and seek the wisdom of the
empty.

★ Stars that light the night, guide me through to
dawn.

*Morpheus:*

★ Not yet, Morpheus; I still have so many things to do.
A little while, and I will accept your beautiful gift.
I'm not rejecting it insultingly:
I simply can't afford to be overwhelmed by such an
amazing present.
Don't worry, though; when I unwrap it,
it'll be that much more appreciated for the
anticipating
and my gratitude that much more.

*Night:*

★ I sit in the night, waiting for dawn,
wrapped in the night , the sister of dawn,
as if I were a child, waiting to be born.

★ Outward sight subdued,
may inward sight grow,
in the night, in the night,
Sister of Dawn.

★  The speckled hen comes to brood
   and light-filled darkness spreads over the earth.
   Silver feathers cover her children with warmth and
       softness,
   like a blanket she covers them.
   With motherly concern she cares for all under her.
   This is you, Night,
   our sweet rescue from the cares of the day.

★  As you come, Night, with stars in your train,
   the crickets begin your song,
   the frogs join in, and the owls too,
   and I, with a human voice,
   praise your overpowering presence,
   all one chorus in your honor.

★  Since even with the stars shining from your body
       you are still dark,
   how can I hope to understand you completely,
       Night?
   I have a small light compared to them, and I am
       only one.
   If you cover me like a blanket that will do.
   What more could you want?

★  First star of evening, be my first guide through
       darkness,
   passing me from one to the rest,
   until morning comes.

# CHAPTER 10

# TIMES OF THE MONTH

The moon is the "measurer." It marks out time in the sky, to the point where ancient people spent a lot of creativity creating calendars that reconciled the unconnected cycles of the sun and the moon. No surprise, really, since it not only tells time; it also controls the tides, and the length of time of a month (a "moon") is that of a woman's reproductive cycle.

Most people think of the moon as female. Not all, however. We have the Man in the Moon, for instance. Most of the prayers in this chapter will be to the female moon, especially in the form of the Wiccan Goddess, but there will be some to a male moon as well.

★ I praise you,
    I praise the Goddess shown in you,
    bright against the dark.

★ Change by continuing law into each phase, one
        following the other,
    from dark, to waxing, to full, to waning, to dark
        again, and once more into growing,
    as I follow your ways, as I submit myself to the same
        laws that govern you.

## Dark Moon

★ New Moon,
  Maiden,
  You are dark now.
  And in the dark, who knows what mysteries are
      enacted?
  For these are women's rites,
  and I, a man, have my own mysteries.
  But I revere them all, and so tonight my thoughts
      are turned to you.
  Lady of Renewal,
  renew the Earth.
  Queen of Darkness, bring in the light.
  Black Void, give birth to the dancing Maiden within me
  and, from her,
  Worlds many and wonderful.

★ I am told by the ways of the Old Ones that this
      darkness is a time necessary for the winning of
      wisdom,
  for its germination, its growth.
  Forgive me my doubt, Moon in your darkness,
  and inspire in me that same germination, that same
      growth,
  that which you yourself possess;
  may I, through my knowledge of you,
  win wisdom.

★   With Her gone from my sight, emptying the sky,
     I, no longer distracted by Her presence outside,
     and no longer excused,
     look within and find Her there,
     find Her light in the darkness,
     find She who changes and remains.
     May I find fullness in the empty.

## New Moon

★   The world begins in darkness,
     and out of darkness springs the light.
     The day begins in darkness,
     and out of darkness comes the dawn.
     The month begins in darkness,
     and in the darkness the new moon is born.
     The Wise One goes into the darkness,
     and returns the Maiden.
     Sweet One of the Silver Crescent:
     We invoke your presence here.
     Come with your fresh love
     and purify your people gathered before you;
     Resurrect us, cleanse us, make us new.

★   Welcome back, little one.
     I've missed you in the days of darkness.
     Welcome back, to adorn the night sky.

★ A new month begins,
   a new moon appears chasing the sun into the dying
      fire of the western sky,
   a new moon dancing an old dance,
   the dance she has always performed,
   the same dance in the same sky,
   the old steps traced in the old pattern by the New
      Moon.
   The Maiden, who is young,
   whose art is skillful, perfected by long years of
      practice,
   a long stream of new moon dances.
   She dances, intent on the spoor of the setting sun,
   dancing Him into his death with Her new life's spirit.
   She dances into death the old,
   dancing into life the new,
   as she appears in the darkening sky of the world, of
      our lives,
   and returns joy to all who lack.

★ I see you in the West, as beautiful as a young child.

★ The Goddess has put her child's artwork on display:
   the sunset sky pinned by the magnet moon to the
      refrigerator of the night sky.

## Waxing Moon

★ As you grow in the sky,
  grow in my soul,
  soft light of the moon.

★ Your increase in size, your increase in light, is
      amazing,
  and that I might see it, and be inspired by it to my
      own growth,
  amazing as well,
  and that's why I'm thanking you.

## Full Moon

★ Blessed be the Goddess of All
  in Her image the Moon.
  Threefold is the Moon
  and threefold we name her.
  When waxing, she is the Maiden.
  Blessed be the Maiden.
  When waning, she is Dark One.
  Blessed be the Dark One.
  But when full, she is the Mother
  and under this name we call her today.
  Come, All-Mother;
  Your people are gathered here:
  Purified, prepared,

properly dedicated to your service.
Come, Mother of All, and shine within us.
Though all else may be dark,
You will be our beacon.
Though all others shall reject us,
You will hold us in your arms.
Though all else be uncertain,
We will place our trust in your wheel of change.
Come, Mother, and be with us.

★  They say there's a Man in the Moon.
And why not; what man, or what woman too,
    wouldn't want to be in the body of the Goddess?
But we already are, we always are.
So says the light of the full Moon tonight.

★  Your milky light, Full Moon Goddess, feeds your
    babies,
your children who rely on you for food to grow.
Pour down each night, Good Mother,
but especially on this one, when you have so much
    to give.

## Waning Moon

★  Old, dark woman,
growing stronger each night
as each night the moon dwindles and we are spun
    slowly but irresistibly into blackness;

you reach out with your sharpening sickled moon,
to divide, and decide,
to cut straight through me and remove any illusions,
any falsehoods and frauds I might harbor,
even unknowingly deep within,
any faults, no matter how dear to my heart.
Please let it be without pain.
But if it has to be painful or frightening,
I'll understand:
the loss of prized possessions is never pleasant,
no matter how necessary or wise.
As your sickle sharpens,
cut ever more finely,
shaping me to approach the person whose perfec-
    tion is appropriate to who I am,
or rather to who I should be,
preparing me for the loss of a light of guidance,
    which will come in the dark of the moon.

★  The sight of the moon may fade:
you will not fade, Goddess.
The light of the moon may fade:
you will not fade, Goddess.
The dark may come and fill the sky
but it will be a wisdom-giving dark:
for it will be your dark, O Goddess.
And you never fade or fail or abandon us,
O Goddess.

★ Goddess Moon, as your cup empties in this time of
     your waning,
   even disappearing into the dark,
   pour your light into me, and I will keep it safe until
     you return,
   and I will pour it back in turn.
   May we be perfect reflections of each other,
   your dark my light,
   your light my dark.

# CHAPTER 11

# TIMES OF THE YEAR

Perhaps above all things, Pagans are identified with celebrating the seasons. We attempt to put ourselves in alignment with the cycle of life and death, of flowers and food, of plants and animals, that follow them. In this way, we seek to make our lives those of nature.

Most modern Pagans follow the eight-festival year of Wicca. This is a combination of the solar festivals (the solstices and equinoxes) and the four great Irish festivals (also called the cross-quarters, since they are found roughly halfway between the solar ones). Other Pagans, particularly Reconstructionists, follow the traditions of other ancient cultures.

I've included several prayers for each of the eight festivals. However, if we want to follow the seasons, we need to follow those of the place where we live. I therefore suggest adapting the prayers to line up with the seasons rather than the days. I also suggest celebrating days other than the eight. I've accordingly included prayers for other occasions, including ones that were not celebrated by those who devised the eight-festival year.

★   Somewhere in this world,
    at some time,
    this day of the year must have been sacred to some
        gods or goddesses.

If I don't know which ones or why,
don't be insulted, but accept this,
given out of my ignorance but no less sincerely.

★ Holy Ones, whose good-will crowns the efforts of
       everyone who works hard to produce, at any
       season,
   bless those whose livelihood depends upon this one,
   whether it be that which is now beginning or now
       brought to its harvest,
   whether farmers, or fishers, or employees whose
       jobs depend on quarterly profits,
   bless them, bless their work.

★ Let us remember the words of the Goddess, that all
       acts of love and pleasure are her rituals, and let
       us take joy in this holiday.

## Imbolc

★ In Ireland, lambs are being born.
   But what is happening in the world outside *here*?
   Telling the old stories is good, but we need to
       remember that if we are to honor this season, we
       need to know what it really is.
   Goddess of the inside, but also of the tame outside,
   we ask you to remind us of both.
   If we then turn away again, back to your sacred

flames, it will be knowing what's going on beyond them.

★ When spring is truly here at last, may we slide into it unsurprised because of the visions allowed by your inspiring light.

*Brighid:*

★ We pour out milk and set out bread for Brighid, who dwells, a living presence, on our hearth. This is what was done in the old times on this night of Imbolc, and we who keep to the traditions of our Ancestors do it again.

## Spring Equinox

*Dawn:*

★ With fallen fetters, in red-robed splendor, stream forth, Dawn Maiden, return the herds. Come to us, Dawn, as cow, not as mare. Disperse the fog the serpent leaves behind. Come to us, Dawn, as cow, not as mare. With your maidens about you, open the gate. Come to us, Dawn as cow, not as mare. Do not block the gate; may the sun's path be free. Come to us, Dawn, as cow, not as mare, opening the mountain's mouth, pouring forth the white streaming water.

Maiden, Dawn, open the way
for the sun to rise and light the earth.
Stream forth, dawn's light.
Do not hold the sun back, Dawn.
Open your cloak and let her rise;
let her rise,
attended by her maidens.
Let her rise, and illumine the world.

★ Look, the ice cracks!
Hear, the snow melts!
Feel, it grows warm!
Spring arrives,
with the summer's gods in her train.

★ Dawn brings the sun over the horizon's edge
    each morning,
winning for light the battle against darkness.
Dancer, win for us today the battle with the dark of
    the year:
from this day may there be more light than dark.

*Eos:*

★ Out of the too-long darkened east,
come to us, Eos, illumine the land!
Out of the long-extending night,
come to us Eos, illumine the land!
Out of the frigid, empty cold,
come to us Eos, illumine the land!

*Eostre:*

★ Born new each morning, you are always young,
a beautiful girl, a welcome child.
It is with particular joy that we see you again on this
    morning, Eostre,
that is to say, "She Who Rises,"
for your rising today is not just the rising of the day
    but the rising of the year,
not just the day's dawn, but the year's.
The Sun that follows will be magnificent, and our
    praises of Him will be proper.
But He shouldn't get *all* the glory, Dawn Goddess,
    for you come too, announcing that He's
    coming, yes,
but worth a prayer or two of your own.
We therefore break our anticipation and stop a while
    to look at this young girl you are,
Eostre who brings today this day's dawn, which is
    the dawn of the year,
reaching up and rising, red in the eastern sky.

This is the day that ushers in the time of light,
and it is the coming of a girl who brings it:
Persephone, Maiden no more, gives birth to
    the spring.

## Spring

★ Kite aloft on the winds of March,
   carry my prayers to the gods of spring.

*Eostre:*

★ The sky is covered with Eostre's cloak,
   and the ground is covered with her tears.
   She rains down gently on our fields,
   Eostre rains down.
   Rise up, rise up,
   the seed in the ground.
   Rise up with Eostre's warmth.

★ Ground appears—what a wonder!—through the
      snow,
   something not seen for months.
   And from spot to spot, from green to green,
   a trail is growing of dancing feet,
   the path of Eostre, who brings the dawn,
   and now the dawn of spring.

*The Goddess:*

★ May the drops of the spring rain be like the hairs
      of the Goddess brushing the earth as she turns
      her smile upon it to awaken the spring plants.

★ In the peepers' call,
   sing to me of spring,
   Mother of Seasons.

*Mars:*

★ Spear and shield, spear and shield,
  Father Mars, Father Mars,
  Dance the steps, dance the steps,
  Sing the hymn, sing the hymn.
  Bring the spring, bring the spring.
  Spear and shield, spear and shield,
  Dance and sing, dance and sing,
  Pater Mars, Pater Mars.

*Persephone:*

★ Softly,
  softly pushing the flowers up from where you are
        hidden under the earth,
  Persephone,
  you're making a dancing ground ready for your
        return,
  when you will tread softly, softly,
  with your maidens and us.

★ There's a young girl in my fields
  and she's dancing.
  She's dancing lightly through them
  between the shoots of the plants.
  They reach up to her out of love
  and she bends down to bless them.
  There's a young girl in my fields.
   Do you see her?
   Sweet Persephone.

*Sun:*

★ The bright yellow crocus,
   a sun in the grass,
   praises with me the Sun in the sky,
   and I with it.

# Beltane

★ Beltane is a time not for prayer, but to dance and
      sing,
   or to pray by dancing and singing.
   Dance and sing:
   For Beltane!
   For May Day!
   For the coming of summer!

*The God and Goddess:*

★ The Maypole is His phallus descending from the Sky.
   The Maypole is Her grain rising from the Earth.
   The ribbons, multicolored, are Their joy, spreading
      out in all directions.
   The Dancers are all of us, weaving the Universe into
      existence.

★ You share the joy of your marriage bed unashamed,
      Eternal Lovers, with the whole world.
   Each opening flower, each leaf unfolding,
   is your cry of ecstasy.

Each bird or animal mating, each man and woman
    making love,
is not a reflection, pale or otherwise, of your
    lovemaking,
but your lovemaking itself.
Each hug, each handshake, each smile,
between lovers, or family, or friends, or strangers:
children conceived today on this Beltane,
on this happy Beltane.

*Opposing Nature Spirits:*

★  All beings of the air who stand in opposition to us,
eagle and hawk, who carry away our animals,
starlings who eat our seeds,
crows who eat our dead:
here is your part of the offering;
don't trouble us.

All beings of the earth who stand in opposition
    to us,
wolf and coyote who carry off our animals,
rabbits and deer who eat our gardens,
ants and termites who destroy our homes:
here is your part of the offering;
don't trouble us.

All beings of the underworld and water
who stand in opposition to us,

bacteria and viruses that carry away our health,
sharks and jellyfish that drive us from the ocean,
grubs and beetles that feed on our food:
here is your part of the offering;
don't trouble us.

All beings of air, earth, and water
who stand in opposition to us:
we have given you your part of the offering;
don't trouble us.

## Planting

★    I write my desires for growth for my plants on this
        little board
and push it into the earth,
where it will be heard.

*Earth:*

★    Open with eager joy to my planting my seeds in you.

★    I put these seeds as offerings to Mother Earth,
        into Her body,
and will receive thankfully the food she gives in
        return,
will thank Her when I eat.

*The Elements:*

★    In the East, where we honor Air,
I erect this prayer stick with ribbons of blue.

May my plants receive the gases they need to make
   their food from the air.
With each flap of the ribbons my prayer is said.

In the South, where we honor Fire,
I erect this prayer stick with ribbons of red.
May my plants receive the light they need to make
   their food from the fire.
With each flap of the ribbons my prayer is said.

In the West, where we honor Water,
I erect this prayer stick with ribbons of green.
May my plants receive the fluid they need to make
   their food from the water.
With each flap of the ribbons my prayer is said.

In the North, where we honor Earth,
I erect this prayer stick with ribbons of yellow.
May my plants receive the minerals they need to
   form their bodies from the earth.
With each flap of the ribbons my prayer is said.

In the Center, where we honor the mystery of the
   spirit of life,
I erect this prayer stick with ribbons of purple.
May my plants receive the spirit they need to form
   their lives from the nonliving;
from Air, and Fire, and Water, and Earth;
so they can give life to spirit,

the gift spirit most desires.
With each flap of the ribbons my prayer is said.

*Garden Spirits:*

★ Whether these seeds that I press into the ground
    will grow,
and how well,
is in your hands, garden spirits.
Others laugh,
and say it's the sun, and rain, and the richness of the
    soil that will decide.
But didn't I just say that?

★ Here in my garden unseen spirits are dancing.
In my moment of blindness of you
may I hear your kind and crashing feet as they fall in
    seasonal rhythm
in your slow but certain circles.

*Rain Spirits:*

★ From mountain, from clouds, they have come.
The Sacred Spirits, bringing rain, have come.
They speak:
From mountain, from clouds, we have come.
We, Sacred Spirits, bringing rain, have come.
To our children who pray to us, we have come.
Plant your seeds now, the rain will come.
Plant corn and beans now, the rain will come.

Plant grain and vegetables now, the rain will come.
Pray to us, children, and we will come.
We speak:
Sacred Spirits, we will pray and you will come.

*Storm God:*

★ Strike with sure aim the waiting earth.
Split with firm stroke the meadows wide.
With blazing axe, with shining blade,
With swift-descending shaft of fire,
prepare and open the fields below
and sow your seed that ours may grow.

## Summer's Beginning

*The All-Gods:*

★ On this day of cold when it should be warm,
at the beginning of summer,
I ask not to doubt that the Gods know what they're
doing,
that the weather is as it should be.
Even so, I pray for summer's warmth.

## Father's Day

*Father Gods:*

★ May all the fathers of the Gods bless all the fathers
of men on this Father's Day.

## Midsummers

★ With the sun's fire at its highest point I immerse
    myself in water,
  at the beginning of the month of the crab.

  *The God:*

★ Long have you grown,
  strong, and hard, and true,
  reaching up from the dark Below until your branch-
    fingers grasped the sun:
  You, reaching You,
  strength holding brightness,
  power, burning,
  standing in unsullied glory.
  Roots snake deep into the darkness.
  You spread these too, just as your branches;
  those seen, these hidden;
  those fed, and these feeding;
  You basing your body on the Below.
  Your branches reach up, pulling your body with
    them,
  the roots reach down, pulling on your body as well.
  It is time.
  Standing in Your glory, the branches and the sun,
  can you feel the pull downward?
  The Dark has its turn.

You needed the darkness to feed your light, but
    nothing is free.
It is time to pay, to fill the hungry darkness,
that pulls you down into death.
A true king does not go on the journey into darkness
    alone;
he must be accompanied by an honor guard.
This is yours, Oak King:
You go with the Four,
You go with the Five.
I give them their marching orders:
Air, when he is in the great emptiness, be his breath.
Fire, when he is in the great cold, be his warmth.
Water, when he is in the great dryness, be his
    moisture.
Earth, when he is in the great stillness, be his
    sustenance.
And you, Spirit, when he is in the great death, be his
    life.
Stand around in protection, you Four,
protecting the body of the Oak King until the
    expected time of growing.
Dwell within, Spirit, protecting his life until the
    expected time of growing:
in the time of fading away, do not let him forget.
These are your orders, you Four, you Five.

You may sink into the darkness,
Oak with the Sun in Your Branches,
with your honor guard about you.

*Sun:*

★  Stand still just a moment in the sky, Sun.
Tarry just a moment in the heavens, King.
Wait just a while on the horizon, Lord.
Stay awhile in balance with dark before the tide
    turns toward it,
and receive my offering.
Know this:
A lord without a throne is still a lord.
A king without a crown is yet a king.
And a sun, even in the time of the year when He is
    absent from the sky more than He is in it, is ever
    a Sun,
and deserves my honor.
Welcome and dear Sun, Lord and King, know this:
through the dark half of the year you will never want
    for worship.
I shall give you deserved gifts.
I shall praise your magnificence.
And I shall pour out heart, words, and deeds in con-
    tinuing worship.

★  Stop for a moment, Sun, your burning and turning
    wheel's rolling.

Stop to smile down with love and approval on the
Earth spread broad beneath you.

Smile as you have done since Her birth, billions of
years ago, when She formed from the random
tumbling rocks, floating in your gravitational
field;

floating, disorganized, until they joined together
through their *own* gravitational field,

until they formed Her, on whom we stand today,
looking up at you smiling in the sky.

When She was formed, burning and turning wheel,
your loving gaze on Her brought forth life from
the dead rock and barren dust,

life that changed, that evolved into the vast numbers of living things spread out across Her,

all tracing their lives back to that one common
Ancestor whose birth you conceived with your
rays.

And one of those species is our own, this member
of which stands here today, looking up at you,
smiling down on us, we standing here on this
longest day.

Stop for a moment, your wheel that burns, that
turns; stop your rolling,

and stand with us, smiling down on those who smile
up at you.

## Summer

*The God:*

★ The sun in the sky on this too-hot day pours down
    its constant message of your power, Lord.
The cooling comfort of the water I sink myself in
    equally proclaims the power of your Lady.
If I seek Her, please don't see it as disrespect for you,
    but as love of Her.
I will long for you on another day,
and turn to you for the comfort I seek from Her
    today.
Lady of the watery womb, I ask you to welcome me.

*Grass:*

★ I trim you as a stylist trims hair,
grass of my lawn,
to bring beauty, not damage.

*Lleu Llaw Gyffes:*

★ Bright One with the Steady Hand,
who threw so straight, hard, accurately,
hitting the target assigned:
guide my arm today;
give me swift and sure motion
to bring the ball over the plate
when and where, in height, in coverage,
I wish it to be.

## American Independence Day

★ A few days before he died on the 50th anniversary
    of independence, the ailing John Adams received
    a delegation of the town elders. They were there
    to ask for something to be read at the celebra-
    tions. Expecting noble and high-flown words,
    they were shocked at what he gave them. They
    perhaps did not understand how noble it was,
    even if not high-flown. What he gave them was
    not a speech, but a toast. Today, on this glorious
    Fourth, raise your cups and make that toast:
Independency forever!

*Liberty:*
★ The fireworks are roses in the bouquet we're giving
    you, Liberty.
Hear our love in their explosions.
The sounds of delight in the watching crowds are
    your hymns,
our rededication to you, the offering.

## Lughnasad

*Lugh:*
★ The spears of Lugh are standing straight, erect,
    golden, in the wheat fields.
And when we reap them, we cut off their blades
    with our own.

And when we grind them, we soften the sharpness
    of a god to that fit for the nondivine.
And when we eat them, we bring into our lives His
    power,
enlivening us, empowering us, encouraging us to
    thank Him.
And we do:
Lugh, thank you.

★ We are here at the feast of Lugh
to honor, praise, and worship the hero of the gods.
Lugh Lámhfhada
Lugh Samhioldanach
He whose arms extend greatly
He of many arts
May he be pleased with this rite.
May he be our champion
May all our fields and crafts be blessed by him.

★ Defeat the Dark One,
Bright One, Champion,
your spear bright against the darkness,
a thunderbolt in a clear sky.
Chase away hail and heavy rain
and bring safely to harvest
our grain, our hearts.

## Lammas

*The God and Goddess:*

★ I place this loaf before the altar,
as first fruits, as thank-you gift,
to you, Goddess, who sends the grain,
to you, God, who *is* the grain:
cut down and consumed on this holy day,
the feast of loaves.

## Monsoon

*Thunderbird:*

★ From cloud-terrace-topped mountains you fly,
each wing beat a roll of thunder,
rain pouring from your feathers to soak the prayer
    feathers we set up in the earth
to call you here, to welcome you here.
Eagle of Thunder, you come to end this dry time,
its heat become the lightning that flashes from
    your eyes.

## Harvest

★ May prosperity ride your diamond-edged sickle,
Reaper, Harvester,
as it cuts through this season's grains.
I offer this loaf of last year's grain in thanks for this
    year's harvest.

★ I hang this sickle, symbol of the harvest, on my door,
　　　so that each time I come in, each time I go out, I
　　　will be reminded of this sacred time, of how the
　　　gods of growth, and the spirits of the land and
　　　plants, brought us here, to where we have food
　　　to be grateful to them for.

*The God:*

★ The sweeping of the reaper's blade
　cuts quite away your offered head,
　the grain from which is ever made
　when threshed and ground our welcome bread,
　this present that we offer you,
　from last year's harvest, rightly due,
　O Dying God, for whom these words are said.

★ Strike down, god of grain, the grain that stands even
　　　now, golden in the fields,
　even as *you* were struck down, struck down yourself
　　　in That Time,
　once and again, and always again, in this.

## Fall Equinox

★ On one side the light, on the other the dark,
　we stand in this moment of balance.
　I would prefer the light, but the earth begs to differ,
　and, turning about the sun, turns her half on which
　　　I live away,

away into the dark.

I can't help but grant you the power, what use
would it be to resist?

I will go with you then, complaining as little as I can,

into the dark period of the year,

believing your promise that your turning will go on,

and return my half of the world to the light.

★  I offer to the gods of the dark season this fruit of
the light.

*The Goddess:*

★  The world is revolving into the year's dark half.

Now, while it is still bright, we celebrate what summer's warmth has brought us.

When our hearts teeter on a point between happiness and despair,

may we remember this moment,

and how it brought us harvest,

and how it comforted us,

and encouraged us to plant hope's seed in the
waiting earth,

Mother of All.

## Fall

★  May their turning be the beauty of my life's
accomplishment.

May their falling be my letting go of life.
May their raking together be my gathering with the
     Ancestors.
May their rotting into compost be my absorption
     into the Earth.
In their feeding new growth, may I see my own
     rebirth.
Dryads, may the glories of your glories be my
     teachers
in this season of the dying year.

★   Wind, I throw these crumbled leaves to you for toys.
     Make beauty with them and I will watch:
     You and I will share the fun.

★   Leaves that are falling from late autumn's weeping
          trees:
     I praise you.
     Stubble in corn fields, left behind after harvest:
     I praise you.
     Chill of the evening that comes bringing winter:
     I praise you.

★   Cut off from the harvesting of yellow wheat,
     I, who live far from the farms,
     turn instead to the gold of the trees, to the red, to
          the orange,
     that feed my soul with beauty as surely as the grain
          feeds my body.

A Pagan, worshipper of the particular, at home in
    the land I find myself in,
praises, not the far-found fields, but the trees on my
    street.

*Maple trees:*

★ The geese are flying
over the maples,
which I wish to praise.

## Apple Harvest

*The God and Goddess:*

★ The apples which fall like the rain which they drank,
    like the cider that will pour out when their slurry
    is pressed,
would not have been possible without the Goddess,
    Queen of Bees and Flowers.
And none of this would have been possible without
    the God, King of Seeds and Trees.
When I drink the cider that is the blood of life of the
    apples from which it is pressed out,
it is the gift of the Goddess and the God that I drink:
their gift, poured out.

## Samhain

★ The doors to winter open, for chill winds to blow
    through:

      they are the doors through which the dead pass,
         from this world and returning to it this night.

★  End over end in the growing darkness it spins,
      with no light to flash from its whetted edge.
      With no light to flash from its whetted edge,
      it comes as a surprise,
      out of darkness, it comes unseen;
      it comes in silence, it comes unheard,
      until with a thud,
      until with a thud it hits our breasts,
      and transfixes the summer hearts we had not
         believed could die.
      With hardly a hiss of resistance, the sickle of harvest
         cuts away our most beloved moments of past
         warmth.
      From the harvest of grain, it comes to the harvest of
         souls.
      Its silent coming pulls from us a sudden cry, and we
         mourn.
      For the death of the year, we mourn.
      For the death of the grain, we mourn.
      For the death of the light, we mourn.
      And we are shocked to learn that we mourn for
         ourselves:
      we mourn for all our losses:
      we mourn for every love that has passed away,

we mourn for every love that never was,
we mourn for every loss we have ever known,
we mourn for losses yet to be,
we mourn for all we have yet to lose,
we mourn for all dreams we will never realize,
we mourn for the little deaths we have known,
we mourn for the little ones to come,
and we mourn for the great one, which will come at
     the end.
If there is no one who will mourn that passing, all
     will still be well,
for tonight we will have mourned in anticipation.
Tonight we will have mourned our own deaths,
we will have mourned the death of all who mourn
     here with us,
we will have mourned the deaths of all who die,
we will have mourned the deaths even of those who
     die unmourned.
We honor these deaths with our mourning,
which comes in the darkness through which Sam-
     hain's sickle flies,
which sounds through the thud of our shock at its
     arrival,
which rings out in the silence of its cutting,
which is heard after it is silent again,
which is the eternal mourning of eternal, unavoid-
     able loss.

We mourn for all deaths.
We mourn.

★ As our beginnings are in the Ancestors,
so the beginning of the year is with this Samhain.
As we welcome the new year at Samhain,
we welcome the Ancestors.
We invite you to us on this Samhain night,
this year's beginning,
that year's end,
to join us at our table, Blessed Dead,
source of our beginning,
promise of our end.

★ We welcome you, the Honored Dead,
whose lives, now over, led to ours:
Welcome and greetings for those gathered here.

★ Come to us, Spirits of the Dead;
Be honored by our rites,
Be pleased with our offerings.
We invite the dead to join with us around the hearth:
We're one family, so it's their hearth too.
Honored Dead, welcome.

★ Is it cold where you dwell, Honored Dead?
Cold like that I feel when I think of joining you,
of joining you, of joining you, on this cold night?
Cold like that I feel when I think of you joining me,

of joining me, of joining me, on this cold night?
Or do you feast in the warm well-lit halls of the
    Lords of the Dead?
Do you travel through meadowy plains in festival
    clothes, singing merry songs?
And does the cold touch you, too, when you think
    of joining us,
of joining us, of joining us, on this cold night?
When we call you to leave that warm and meadowy
    world do you hesitate,
as we would hesitate to answer *your* call?
Our hall is well-appointed, our feast well-spread,
showing shame to neither host nor guest.
We invite you to it: join us, join us, join us.
Together we will warm this cold night.

★   This cold, dark night is made colder and darker by
    the dead who gather around us.
May they grow brighter, grow warmer, through this
    offering,
may they lap at this milk and be filled with life for
    the time of this ritual
so that they will hear the stories of them that we will
    tell.

## Halloween

★   Tonight the world turns topsy-turvy,
and children in costumes,

hidden behind masks,
roam through the darkness asking for treats.
May you, all you Numinous Ones,
be as open-handed in the coming year as I am
    tonight
to these spirits of misrule ringing my doorbell and
    asking me to give.

## Thanksgiving

★ Here we are, gathered on this wonderful holiday,
    among family and friends,
and all we can think is "thank you."
Thank you to all those whose presence made this
    celebration possible,
and gratitude most of all to the Shining Ones,
whom we will continually praise.

## Planting Winter Wheat

★ Keep safe in your womb this winter wheat,
    Mother Earth;
may the cold which kills so much else be a catalyst
    for its growth.

## Beginning of Winter

★ Facing the winter
with fear, with trepidation,

this time of cruel ice,
we will trust the Gods
and the mighty Ancestors;
we will sing in the darkness,
we will dance in the cold,
and all will be well.

★  As winter closes in,
I will fight the coming cold,
the coming dark,
the death around me.
I will fight for life.
And when I fail, as I will,
may it be with grace.
Summer deities,
spirits of growth and life,
stand by me in my struggle.
Winter deities,
spirits of the hard and the dead,
be good winners.
Teach, don't punish me,
who has only fought for what I love.

*Orion:*
★  Bold Orion on the rise,
see the summer fall before you:
guard us in the growing dark.

# Yule

*Sun:*

★ Though even at noon you are low in the winter sky,
       your glory is worthy of praise,
   and so my prayer.

★ The safely contained fire on the hearth is a herald
       in winter's cold of the power of the summer's
       sun, which will be the outside hearth of the sky.
   The herald has arrived, if not the One who sent it.
   On this midwinter's night, we are here to acknowl-
       edge the message of hope,
   but also to praise and offer to the herald itself,
       whose glorious friendship is itself worth this
       prayer.

★ Each candle we light is a star.
   Let us light as many as we can, and spend time
       among the stars we've created on Earth.
   Let us know that their twinkling is them smiling,
       because they know a secret:
   the Sun will be coming back, and not only return-
       ing, but strengthening,
   from this day through many,
   from this darkest of nights.
   On Yule, let us laugh with the stars at our fear of
       eternal darkness,
   laugh with these earthly stars we've lit.

★  Sink without fear,
   without fear in the west, O Sun,
   without fear of our fear,
   without fear that your children will fear.
   For you will rise again,
   you will arise stronger.
   For you will grow again,
   you will grow stronger.
   The tide is turning again, we have no fear,
   for it's Yule.

## Winter

*The God:*

★  There is beauty in emptiness,
   and in the skeleton of trees against the darkening
       blue of dusk's sky.
   When my teeth chatter in winter's wind, remind me
       of this,
   God who dwells in the dark as well as the light.

*Rain Spirits:*

★  Winter rain, are your drops tears because no one
       praises you?
   Here are my words for your beauty:
   may it be tears of joy you pour down.

*Sun:*

★  All through the growing season it was you whose
       light allowed the growing:

How can we not praise you, here in the darkness?
All through the growing season it was you whose
    heat allowed the growing:
How can we not praise you, here in the cold?
All through the growing season it was through your
    heat and light that there was growing at all:
How then can we not praise you, standing here in
    the cold and darkness,
even as our souls cry for heat and light:
You are found even when hidden.

*Snow Spirits:*

★ Tomorrow I will no doubt curse you as I drive to work.
  I hope you will forgive then, remembering how you
      charmed.

★ First snow, tuck the earth in under your feather quilt,
  keep her safe till spring.

★ On each flake ride
  to the waiting below,
  the whitening world,
  Spirits of Snow.

# CHAPTER 12

# TIMES OF LIFE

Conducting a rite of passage at a special time of life makes it just that—special. It says: "Pay attention, this moment *means* something." But this can be done in mundane ways—birthday candles are blown out, a marriage license is signed, an obituary is written and published. A rite of passage does more. It creates the change it observes. It changes the person who undergoes it. It calls upon the power of the divine to make the person a different one. If a secular tradition whispers, "This is special," a sacred ritual "hits you up side the head."

Most of the prayers in this chapter aren't intended to be used by themselves. They belong embedded in a longer ritual, perhaps one constructed of other prayers in this book. They can make a secular wedding sacred or they can make a wake a Pagan one. Most of all, they can make a new person.

★ Each moment of my life, born and dying away,
  I place in offering on your altar, All-Gods.

## Birth

★ Which of you Gods, which of you Goddesses,
  have helped bring this child into our world?

Whether one, or a few, or many, or all,
even if I don't know which ones you are, I thank you;
those who should receive my thanks, please do.

★　May your pockets never be empty,
may your hands never be closed.
May you receive graciously,
may you give gladly.
May you be a pleasure to know,
may you always be among friends.
Long life, happy life,
beautiful life, useful life.
We bless you today:
may you always be blessed.

*The God:*

★　A father's love seems hard,
Father of All,
but is freedom to do,
is challenge to act.
As you open before my child life's responsibility
walk beside [her/him] as Guide.

*The Goddess:*

★　Seeing the child to whom I have given birth
I think of you, forever giving birth to all.
You are the perfect mother, even with so many
　　children.

May I be as perfect a mother to this one child,
never achieving that goal,
but finding in it not despair but dedication.

★ You who give birth to all things, living and
      nonliving,
this child of yours offers this child of yours to you.

*Helios:*

★ Open your eyes, little child,
"Open them," is the prayer of Helios, who lights the
      world.
Open your eyes to the beauty of your life.

## Naming

★ We welcomed you to life.
We welcomed you to birth.
We welcomed you to your family.
And now, by giving you this name, we welcome you
      to society.
This will be how you will introduce yourself to
      others:
"Hi, my name is [name],"
and they will reply,
"Hi, [name]; glad to meet you."
So this is what we are saying today:
"Hi, [name]; glad to meet you."

★   We give you the name [name], little one,
    such a big gift for such a little person.
    Though you are too young to accept it yourself,
    and to thank its givers,
    your parents accept it in your stead,
    this name given in love,
    by those who look forward to your hearing it
        joyfully.

★   With this word, with your name, [name],
    we weave you into the web of words, which
        together sing the love of the God and Goddess.

*The Goddess:*
★   You give birth, and know the pains and joys of
    bringing children into the world.
    You watch us grow, and know the worries parents
        share for their children.
    You bless all in general with the protection a mother
        brings.
    Bless this child in particular, whom we bring to you
        today to be given a name,
    Goddess, lover of children.

★   May your name be a bead in the necklace of souls
        around the neck of the Great Goddess,
    decorating Her beauty,
    adding to it its own.

## First Day of School/Graduation

★ Brighid, and Ogmios, and Apollo, and Hermes, and
       Tahuti, and Vāc:
   and all the deities
   and all the Ancestors,
   all who guide children in learning.
   Whether I know you and have worshipped you,
   Whether *anyone* has known you or ever worshipped
       you,
   today's offerings are for you,
   to ask you to guide this child in [his/her] education
       from this day/to thank you for your guidance of
       this child on [his/her] graduation day.

## School

★ Your pencils the spears of Lugh,
   your lunch the fire of Brighid,
   your notebooks the tablets of Oghma.
   Go to school with the gods,
   go to school with the blessings of the gods,
   go to school under their protections.

## Coming of Age

★ We have raised this child to be a worthy
       [man/woman],

one who accepts responsibilities acquired.
We have raised this child to be a worthy [man/
    woman]

★    Look upon the deities of your home one last time.
    [pause]
    Don't worry, this isn't really the last time.
    For the rest of your life you will often return to them.
    But it will be different; it will be as if returning to a
        home you once lived in,
    feeling welcomed, and enjoying the memories,
    but knowing it is not really yours anymore.
    Offer this last time to the deities of that time, thank-
        ing them for what they have done for you.
    [offering]
    They won't all be staying. Many will come with you,
        even though your relationship will change. Offer
        to them and invite them to come along.
    [offering]
    Turn away toward your future now.
    There is a threshold in front of you. No matter what,
        and no matter when, you will have to cross it.
    The question is, will you be dragged, or will it be
        willingly?
    If it is willingly, offer to the god of the threshold, and
        then step across boldly, with your right foot, to
        enter a new life rightly.

★  No one asked you if you wanted to grow up:
   Nature forced you.
   But now, each day you will choose how to fulfill this
      new-acquired responsibility.
   Don't blame Nature, but thank Her, for the unimagi-
      nable gift She's forced on you,
   the gift of something to match yourself against,
   the gift of a challenge to meet.
   Relax, though; I know you can do it.

★  I went over the top first, to clear the way for you.
   I yelled, "Follow me!" and you did.
   You've followed me long enough:
   go on ahead.
   It's as safe as it's going to be.
   I'll watch your back, I'll be covering you.
   It's as safe as it's going to be.
   Go on ahead with my blessing promise.

## Wedding

★  [name], look into her eyes.
   [name], look into his.
   From the beginning of humanity Man has looked
      into Woman's eyes,
   and Woman has looked into Man's,
   and seen the same thing.

Each of you look carefully into each others' eyes
    today,
and each day that you live see what you see today
and what has always been there since the
    beginning.

★  You might think that you've come here as
    individuals, but hoping to be made one.
And so, if your vows are true, you will be.
But you aren't just individuals:
you are every man and woman.
So when you become one, every man and woman
    are made one,
and those watching here aren't just present because
    they love you,
but as representatives of all men and of all women.
In your becoming one, they are made one.
This day is yours, but not yours alone,
it belongs to all humanity, living and dead.
Don't think that this makes you less important:
it makes you more.
You are individuals, and nothing is taken from that.
Your love, and your need to be married, are admired
    by everyone here;
and everyone here is grateful to you as well;
to you as individuals,
willing, by your love today, to join all humanity
    together,

in the eternally renewing and mysterious unity that
    is our species.

★   Join hands,
    Join hearts,
    Join lives,
    Join voices in prayer with those who love you,
    gathered here on this happy day.

*The God and Goddess:*

★   God and Goddess, Husband and Wife:
    May this marriage be strong.
    May this marriage be long-lasting.
    May this marriage be productive.
    May this love be true and truly made,
    as is yours, Eternal Lovers,
    Goddess and God.

★   As the God and Goddess you join together:
    two to each other, and one to all who see you,
    and in the life you will live,
    you, joining together in our witness today.

## Death

★   May I enter the Great Dark with eyes open,
    the Great Silence, singing.

★   There will be a time, Old Woman,
    when I will see your face, Old Woman,

at the right time, Old Woman,
and not before.
[pause]
And then, Old Woman, I will likely be terrified.
All change is frightening,
so the greatest change of all must be the most
    frightening of all.
More terrifying still is that you *know*.
You know the terror you will bring, but you still
    come.
How cruel can you be?
But most terrifying of all is what I will see in your
    face:
love.
You come bringing terror and love.
True compassion might mean death.
[pause]
So I ask you now, Old Woman,
when I am not looking in your eyes, Old Woman,
that when the time comes, Old Woman,
I might see beyond the terror into your love.
Old Woman.

★ The stubborn leaves of oaks cling to their branches,
    until their successors are ready to open green.
    Death, for my children's sake,
    give me more time,

until I am no longer needed,
and then take me, willing;
gladly I'll go with you then,
to rest after long work.
But for now I am needed here.

★  When it is right for me to enter your kingdom,
   Lord of Death, Gatherer of Souls,
   May I go gently.
   May I be a leaf dropping from a tree.
   May I be a snowflake falling from the clouds.
   May I be a drop of dew drying in the light of dawn.
   Like opening my hands, like letting go,
   Like one final gift:
   May it be like that.

## Funeral

★  May your soul take a soft-footed journey,
   on a soft-floored path through the old forest
   to the Land of Comfort,
   where the only tears are the drops of rain falling
        from leaves,
   the only moaning deep ocean swells,
   the only sighing light evening breezes.
   Rest in that land, with the peace you have earned.

*For this prayer, trace a circle on the corpse's forehead with a paste made from wet powdered red chalk:*

★   I anoint you with the red of blood: may the blood of
          life return to you in that other world.
     I anoint you with the wet: may the suppleness of
          water return to you in that other world.
     I anoint you with the sun: may the warmth of the
          sun return to you in that other world.
     I anoint you with a red, moist sun: may life return to
          you in that other world.

★   To the person who has died, we say:
     "Peace between us; go on your way with our
          blessings."
     To those who have come here for farewells, we say:
     "Peace among us; may we live blessed together."

★   In the Shining Land,
     lit and warmed by the sacrificial fires,
     around the sea that teems with life,
     all the Ancestors, wise and loving,
     wait, patiently but expectantly,
     for your arrival.
     They will greet you, their friend,
     and among all those who have come to that place,
     you will live, and rest,
     until the time comes for once again taking up
          a body.

You know the pain of life, you have suffered the pain
    of death,
and you know the joy of life, the love and beauty,
and even the wondering in awe before the storms
    you've faced.
With the farewells of those you have lived among,
Under the blessing of the Lord of that land,
By the unfailing direction of the Guide who brought
    you there:
return among the people of the earth,
once again bringing happiness.

★  His boat's keel scrapes on the beach's shingle.
    Leaping from the prow, he is home,
    finally home,
    where his life began and where it will begin again.

*Agni:*

★  Like butter in the flames
    this body in the fire,
    bring, Agni, into glory:
    this one of our people.

*The Goddess:*

★  His whole life has been like waiting and growing
    in your womb.
    The time has come for his birth, from this world into
    another.

Bring him, Goddess, through the pangs of this new
    birth,
there into that other world.
Hold your baby there, draw him close to you, feed-
    ing him with inexhaustible milk from your ever-
    giving breasts.
Rock him in your soothing arms, until he knows the
    peace of a baby resting in his complete faith in
    his mother.

*Osiris:*

★  In the Land of the Dead,
    with the trials passed,
    with the dangers overcome,
    with my heart weighed and found true,
    I will be reborn as Osiris.

# CHAPTER 13

# ENDINGS

As I said in chapter 2, a ritual has a beginning, a middle, and an end. The end must undo the beginning, and so the prayers for it are the reverse of the beginning, and are spoken in the reverse order. The ritual "unwinds," and we find ourselves where we were before. Even if we have been transformed by our encounter with the sacred, we are humans, and we live in a human world, and that is the world to which we must return.

We say good-bye to the Holy Ones, we dismantle our sacred space, and we say good-bye to each other. And so the ritual ends.

## Separations

★ Return, return, from these changing rites.
  Return, return, to your daily life.
  Return, return, and with fresh eyes see the world.

★ These rites are over,
  this time in sacred time,
  this gathering in sacred space.
  We go now to our everyday lives,
  but transformed by our experience of the sacred:
  the profane less profane,

the mundane less mundane,
the everyday less everyday,
to our newly opened eyes.

★ It's always hard to leave a place.
But that which is left is not left behind;
it comes with us as we go,
and never leaves us,
though days and miles do their best.

★ Our time here is done.
We have worked.
We have worshipped.
We have been in the Land of the Gods
and rejoiced in their presence.
It is good that we have done this.
But now we must return to our land,
the same, but changed by the blessing of the Holy
    Ones.

★ Hear me, O people:
You have done well.
The gods are pleased
and have granted their blessings.
Go now in peace and know they are with you.
Peace, blessed be.

★ Each outward breath a step from their world.
Each inward breath a step toward our own.

But each beat of our hearts their continuing pres-
    ence within us.
Though far way, they are with us now,
and will continue to be so,
securing our lives with each beat of our hearts.

★  The sand castle dissolves when the tide comes in.
    The ice sculpture melts with warming air.
    Our circle dissipates with the ending of our rites.
    Each remains in the minds of their creators
    and in the minds of all who have known them.
    All gone.
    All still here.

★  All we are will be the Goddess,
    All we do will be the God.
    Transformed by them, but still ourselves,
    we will live our lives more truly,
    and we will come to them again,
    pulled by the need for them which glows in the
        hearts of our souls.

## Farewell

★  Holy Ones, Shining Ones, You whose power is great,
    though you go on your way, may it never be said
        that we have lacked anything in our worship,
    that we have not honored you as you deserve.

★ Farewell to you, to you who shine,
   you, immortal ones, Givers of Gifts,
   farewell, good friends,
   blessers of those who worship you,
   who invite you to their table,
   who share with you their best,
   their libations lovingly poured.

★ As we called them facing East,
   we say farewell facing West.
   As the sun they rose,
   as the sun they set,
   as the sun they will rise again in our lives
   when we ask them to come to us.

★ Turn in silence, in your minds, in your innermost
      hearts,
   to say good-bye to those we have worshipped.
   Turn, and with the mind's clear voice, say farewell to
      those we have worshipped.
   Turn again your thoughts and attention to those we
      have been well and truly worshipped,
   and now, aloud, and with love,
   say "Farewell!"

★ Go forth, return home,
   each footfall a prayer to those who have blessed you,
   each turn of your car's wheels one with Nature's
      turning,

each means of travel a continuation of the sweet
    blessing
of those we have honored here.

★ All the sacred beings who have shared time with us
    today,
have shared in our meal,
have received the offerings we have given with
    hearts of gratitude,
have heard the words of praise we have spoken,
the songs of beauty we have sung:
we wish you well, departing guests,
on your way from our home to yours.
Go as friends, who, as we well know, are great in
    hospitality,
whose ready invitations to your well-famed feasts we
    await eagerly,
happy to come when called,
to receive with gratitude your inevitable gifts,
and to invite you to come again to dine with us.

★ You go now to your homes,
our friends,
from this place of celebration.
We go now to our homes,
your friends,
from this place of celebration.

As friends we have shared this time,
as friends enjoyed this party together,
as friends celebrated these rites,
each one doing what friends do when they get
　　together.
We will celebrate again,
as friends do,
here, or elsewhere,
always in a place of celebration.

★ The sun sets, and it is night.
The moon sets, and it is dark.
The frost falls, and it is cold.
But when you come,
there is day, and light, and warmth.
When we call to you from the greatest depths of our
　　lives,
we know that you will come to us from love and
　　friendship.
And with this knowledge, we say good-bye to you,
all you Holy Ones.

★ Has what I have done here pleased you?
Then please me with what I have asked for.
Has what I have given been welcome?
Then give me what I have asked for.
It is only fair, and you are fair.

★ Spirits who have spent this time with us,
  we know it is now time for you to return to your
      homes,
  and you know this too:
  this is our last knowing-together.
  We give you this food,
  to keep you strong on your journey.
  We give you this drink,
  to quench your thirst.
  We give you these words,
  to lighten the way.
  With gifts and words, we give our farewell,
  to you, Revered Ones,
  who have blessed us today.
  As you go on your way, you go with our thanks.

*The God and Goddess:*

★ We leave with their blessings:
  With the Goddess beside us,
  even though we leave.
  With the Goddess within us,
  even though we leave.
  With the God beside us,
  even though we leave.
  With the God within us,
  even though we leave.
  With the Divine Pair beside us,

even though we leave.

With the Divine Pair within us,

even though we leave.

We leave with their blessings.

*Land Spirits (perhaps throw a handful of grain with each "Return." May also be used as a litany):*

★ Return to mountain and river:

you know the way.

Return to forest and field:

you know the way.

Return to desert and scrub:

you know the way.

Return to rock, to tree and bush and grass,

to animal, and insect, and bird:

you know the way.

Return, return, return to these, your homes:

you know the way.

Return, return, return to us when we call from our
     need:

May you know the way.

## Sacred Space

★ We ask from the East the gifts of the East.

We ask that they become us.

We ask from the South the gifts of the South.

We ask that they become us.

We ask from the West the gifts of the West.
We ask that they become us.
We ask from the North the gifts of the North.
We ask that they become us.
From each direction we ask the proper gift
to bring with us as we leave this place.

★ Spirits of Air, go on your way,
to your home, to that blesséd realm,
leaving blessings behind in the peace between us.

Spirits of Fire, go on your way,
to your home, to that blesséd realm,
leaving blessings behind in the peace between us.

Spirits of Water, go on your way,
to your home, to that blesséd realm,
leaving blessings behind in the peace between us.

Spirits of Earth, go on your way,
to your home, to that blesséd realm,
leaving blessings behind in the peace between us.

★ I smooth out the break between this world and the
        next,
zipping it up,
sewing together the halves of this seamless garment
        of the world we love.

*Pour milk into a bowl and cast it as an offering in the directions as noted.*
*(This prayer is complemented by an opening prayer found in chapter 1:*

★   We stand, pillars, in the center of the world,
     while all else turns about us.
     In the Center, Cosmos gifts Chaos.
     It gifts it with order and with peace.
     May there be peace in the South
     May there be peace in the West
     May there be peace in the North
     May there be peace in the East,
     the place of prayer, the place of light,
     the place of the Holy Ones.
     And may there be peace in the Center,
     where we stand, pillars,
     while all else turns about us.

★   A home is sacred ground,
     where gods dwell.
     So we do not return from sacred ground,
     where gods dwell.
     We remain on sacred ground,
     where gods dwell.
     Those gods who have come to be with us in this
          home,
     where gods dwell,
     believe us when we say that you will always be wel-
          come in this home,

where gods dwell.
Gods of this home,
believe that we are glad you dwell here.
And we show our belief, and our love as well,
with this poured-out milk and offered bread,
showing our happiness at living in a home,
where gods dwell.

★ The space which we have transformed from profane
    to sacred
we transform from sacred to profane again.
losing nothing thereby of the sacred gifts the divine
    beings have conveyed to us,
losing nothing of the knowledge of the mysteries we
    have acquired,
losing nothing of the memories of that blesséd land
    which lies beyond ours,
which supports and sustains.
May those gifts,
may that knowledge,
may those memories,
support and sustain us as we go about our everyday
    lives:
We are those who have dwelt in the sacred land
and will again.

# PART III:

## PETITIONING THE GODS

*The work part of a ritual can vary greatly. We've seen some of the major purposes a ritual can have in Part II. There are many others, however—some personal and not suited to group ritual, and some more appropriate to occasions when the rest of a ritual needs to be simplified, or even eliminated; while driving, perhaps, or waiting on the tarmac, or upon seeing an ambulance go by. Others, like divination, can be parts of rituals dedicated to other purposes. Most of the prayers in this section are written so they can stand alone or be part of a more complete ritual. I've given them their own section*

to make it easier to find prayers for specific occasions without cluttering up the main ritual part of the book.

Another reason for giving these prayers their own section is that they are petitionary—that is, they ask for something specific. Some of the prayers in Part II are also petitionary, but petitioning is the main purpose of the prayers in this section; petitioning is what they are all about.

I've organized the prayers by intent. Because of the overlap of purposes, I've combined more than one in some chapters. For instance, many travel prayers are for safety, so I put them in the chapter on safety.

The idea of petitionary prayers may seem a selfish one. In a sense they are, but it is our personal relationships with the deities that are being relied on in them. "Selfish" is not perhaps the right term; "centered on one's own problems" is better.

Petitionary prayers don't have to be for your own problems, of course. At their most basic, your concerns are tied in with those of others. The rain you pray for will benefit other farmers; peace will be a gift to everyone; justice is a requirement for a good society.

Some petitionary prayers are specifically for others. Prayers for healing or prayers for comfort, for instance. These prayers can easily be adapted for the benefit of other people simply by changing "me" to "this person," "my friend," "my patient," "all humanity," or someone specified by name.

Still, most of the prayers in this section of the book center around the well-being of the person praying. It's been like that for millennia, and self-interest is still the most common intent for spontaneous prayers.

# CHAPTER 14

# GENERAL REQUESTS
# AND OFFERINGS

We can ask the divine beings for just about anything. This chapter give prayers for some of these wide-ranging needs. It also includes prayers that can be used to prefix others. Here you will find prayers that don't fit into any of the other chapters but don't have purposes large enough to merit their own. Here you will also find prayers that are general, in the sense that more specific intentions can be attached to them.

★ We have been hosts today, and know you will be
    ours in the future.
It's been this way at least as long as there have been
    people,
and will continue to be,
even those who have forgotten you treating each
    other in the sacred way you and we do.

★ When I speak, may it be divine words.
When I think, may it be divine thoughts.
When I act, may it be divine deeds.
May what I do be divine.
May what I am be divine.
May I be divine, be divine.

★ My divine self asks my divine self to remember itself.

★ The first offering I make is the life of this wood.
  I offer to that offering with this offering,
  [oil/butter] to feed you.

★ Giver[s] of Gifts,
  I give in return,
  with reverent heart,
  this [offering].

★ With this gift, I maintain my relationship with the
      Gods.
  With this gift, I maintain my relationship with the
      Ancestors.
  With this gift, I maintain my relationship with the
      Land Spirits.
  With gift and with gift, relationships are established
      and maintained.

★ Each of you has your gift,
  and each your preferred offerings.
  Since I can't give everything,
  I give you this,
  asking for gifts from those who are pleased by it.

★ Refreshed by this drink, find power and reason to
      help [me, us, etc.] to [petition].

★ I'm not trying to buy your affection with this, but to
      show you mine.

★ I pour out words of praise to you with this drink.
  I remember you;
  remember me when I need you.

★ With [these words/this offering/etc.], I pray to you
    today, [god's name].
  I have prayed to you in the past, and will praise you
      in the future.

★ All the Holy Ones, be honored in our midst.
  We pour out our offering to you,
  like living water,
  like grain from a bag.
  Drink deeply of the gifts we give.

*Aengus Óg, for love:*

★ Aengus Óg, young lad, young son,
  Though I am no longer young,
  may love grow in my old heart.

*Agni:*

★ May Agni, priest of the gods,
  carry this offering to them.

★ Each of your tongues speaks a word;
  a thousand tongues, a thousand words;
  a thousand words, a single prayer;
  a single prayer, through our offering,
  convey to the gods as you rise,
  Agni who prays to us,
  god of prayer, priest to the gods.

*Agni, with an offering of butter:*

★    May this be to you as food, Agni;
Agni, may this be to you as drink.
Priest of the gods, go,
strengthened by my offering, to them,
carrying my prayers in your hands,
speaking them with your mouth.

*The All-Gods:*

★    It's not really so hard to see the gods, is it?
You open your eyes and there they are.
But I'm fooling myself if I think that seeing you is
    enough.
My deepest of gazes won't go deep enough to see
    all of you.
You are truly amazing, all of you.
The least among you is incomprehensible.
You are a different kind from me.
But are we so different?
We can meet as friends over the offering.
Perhaps you will be the greater,
but we will be friends nonetheless.
Look what I have brought for you:
here is food.
Let's sit down and eat together like friends do.
Someday I will sit at *your* table.
Today, sit at *mine.*

★ You set before us a banquet, All-Gods,
   and we ask for table-scraps.
   Today my prayer is "Open my eyes."

   *Ancestors:*

★ Ancestors, listen to me—
   Remember how you prayed to *your* ancestors?
   Well, now I'm praying to *you.*
   Your prayers were respectful and so are mine.
   Your prayers were for favors and so are mine.
   I only expect what you expected
   and what others will expect of me when I join you.
   Family help family.

★ Ancestors, whose death has brought you close to
        the gods,
   bring these prayers of mine, these offerings of mine,
        to them, without losing any along the path there,
   and in the same way, bring their gifts to me.
   Take some part of these offerings in payment for
        your services, and some part of the divine gifts
        as well.

   *Aphrodite, for love:*

★ Born of foam, where water and air meet,
   you bring together woman and man in loving
        embrace.
   Lovely Aphrodite of golden sandals,
   bring someone to love to me.

My happiness will be as great as that which is right
    to mortals
if you answer my prayer,
that of me, who burns this incense in your honor:
sweet smell for the sweetest one.

*Brighid:*

★ Brighid, Brighid, fire.
Brighid, Brighid, poet.
Brighid, Brighid, healer.
Brighid, Brighid, smith.

Inspiring one, Brighid, Brighid.
Loving one, Brighid, Brighid.
Welcoming one, Brighid, Brighid.
Protecting one, Brighid, Brighid.

Brighid, who guards children, Brighid.
Brighid, who warms the homeless, Brighid.
Brighid, who watches over the helpless, Brighid.
Brighid, who enwraps the bereft, Brighid.

Brighid, Brighid, hear our prayers;
our prayers hear, Brighid, Brighid.
Your children call upon their mother,
upon their mother, Brighid,
upon you, Brighid, Brighid,
upon you,
upon you, Brighid.

*Fire:*

★ The grass grows from the rotted death in the earth.
The cow eats the grass and makes milk for her calves.
The milk contains the cream, and the cream the
    butter,
and the butter contains this fuel that shines with the
    sun's gold
and with which we feed you,
fire of transformation.

*The God:*

★ If I should hesitate to approach your altar,
there in the hiding shadow of threatening pines,
the pillars of your cathedral:
Know that I am more afraid of what might be lost
than desiring of what might be gained.
Lord of Light, here Lord of Shadow,
show me the light in the shadow,
teasing me from my ignorance,
and from my fear.

★ We sing in praise of the God of Help;
we sing with words finely wrought,
we sing with thanks for all His blessings,
we sing to Him just as we ought,
we sing for all His gifts freely given,
we sing for His lessons well-taught.

*The God, for a building under construction:*

★  With this flag-decked tree, I top this structure,
   its skeleton done,
   its flesh yet to be completed.
   Lord of heights,
   Lord of trees,
   Lord of all that stands erect:
   we pray for safety in our construction.

*The God, for strength:*

★  Lord of strength, give me strength;
   to your faithful friend, strength.

*The God and Goddess:*

★  With the love of the God,
   be blessed, be blessed.
   With the love of the Goddess,
   be blessed, be blessed.
   With the love of the God and of the Goddess,
   be blessed, be blessed.
   With Their love, may you be blessed,
   be blessed, be blessed.

*The Goddess:*

★  With well-deserved reverence, I pour with open
      hands this honoring gift on your holy land,
   you who are our Lady, our Mother, our granter of
      happiness.

*Green Man:*

★ From the tree leaves eyes are peering, smiling.
But when I turn my back, it seems like they're look-
    ing with distrust.
So I leave this for the Green Man to prove my good
    intentions.

*Hermes, for advice:*

★ Trickster whose cleverness defeated Apollo, the
    wisest of gods,
except for Zeus,
and amused Zeus himself, father of men:
show me the way out of this predicament,
bring me a clever solution.

*Hermes, during a negotiation:*

★ Herald of Zeus, you bring together one and another;
as a small child, you gained through your cleverness
    the friendship of Apollo,
with whom you were at enmity.
So too, bring this conflict to a peaceful resolution
by finding that thing each one desires and the other
    is willing to give,
and conveying that knowledge to us,
to we who are negotiating.

*Herakles, for strength:*

★ Strength in my limbs, Heroic Herakles,
give me for the task ahead,
for successful labors.

*Jupiter:*

★ Iupiter Optimus Maximus
Jupiter, Best and Greatest
From your seat above the sky
Look down to me.
Smell the sweet scent rising to you.
Hear the holy words reaching to you.
Answer my prayer, Most Holy One.

*Land Spirits:*

★ I don't bring incense:
you have incense already—leaves and needles
underfoot.
I don't bring libations:
you have libations already—streams and springs in
the depths.
I don't bring sacrifices:
you have sacrifices already—the deaths of plants and
animals in your hidden places.
I've brought instead something you don't already
have:
prayers spoken in human words,
prayers are my gift.

★ With the help of the Land Spirits,
whom I will continue to honor,
may this construction project run smoothly.
May it be finished on time and within budget.

*Life:*

★   My heart the fire of offering.
My flesh and bones the offering.
My blood the libation.
But whom to offer to?
To life this continual offering,
on this day,
on all days,
in thanks and love.

*Lugh, against opposition:*

★   A spear with flames streaming like waves of a brazen
        sea in ripples along its length
appears before the eyes of my mind, my heart, my
        soul,
held by a man whose face shines with the brilliance
        of a flowering sun,
from whose fingertips and from each hair on whose
        head leap bold lightning strikes,
jagged scythes through the Cosmos that strike down
        all who oppose him,
each flash like the spear he holds, of stiff and flowing
        molten bronze,
which he will direct with his sure arm to its true target.
Lugh, you know the target I have in mind,
the walls, and those who man them, who stand in
        my way,
who press on me with many threats to my own true
        actions:

as you are true, and your aim, so am I and my
purpose.

And that is why I dare ask you to loose your spear
against my adversaries.

Help one who will be properly grateful,
speaking of the power you wield in gatherings
of men.

*Maat, for proper action:*

★ The justice that you rule, Maat,
O Queen of the Feather,
is not just that of the courtroom,
is not, in fact, *primarily* that of the courtroom.
It is, rather, the justice of the life well-lived.
The slightest ill-wrought deed disturbs the balance.
May my life be such that it matches your justice
perfectly;
may none of my actions be such that I would be
ashamed for my heart to be placed in the pan of
your scale,
opposite your feather of the truly acted life,
Maat whose judgment is true.

*Manannán mac Lir, for consolation for a lost love:*

★ Your cloak, Manannán, mist of the sea,
which separated Fand from Cú Chulaiin,
removing them from the pains of a doomed love;
place it between me and [name], my lately loved one,
from whom I am now parted forever.

*Marduk, for protection against enemies:*

★ This is a story of what happened before anything
        happened,
    when Tiamat rose against the gods,
    the great emptiness threatening to swallow them all.
    The gods, defeated, huddled fearfully in their shin-
        ing halls.
    Desperate, they turned to the great champion,
    the caster of the thunderbolt,
    supreme in war:
    Marduk!
    They prayed to him for help.
    Can you imagine it, the gods praying?
    In fear the great ones came to him,
    asking him to save them from the Great Deep.
    The Roaring One, with lightning playing around his
        head,
    the Arrogant One,
    agreed with their prayer.
    He promised to save them,
    but asked something in return.
    (He deserved it, he who was to set his face against
        all-encompassing darkness.)
    This is what he asked:
    the kingship of all, gods and men.
    He did not, actually, ask this:
    he *demanded* it, as would only be fair for one who
        could stand up to the Abyss.

And how could the gods refuse him?
They of great might were cowering in fear,
dreading the smothering sea,
greatly fearing Tiamat;
how could they say no?
They gave it to him, then,
the kingship,
the lordship over gods and men.
With relief they put it into his hands,
singing in joy for the strength of Marduk.
He took up his mace and set forth.
Terrible was he to see.
Humans could not have borne the sight,
so strongly did the light of heaven shine from him.
His mace was lightning, his feet shook heaven.
With his quick-striking mace he lashed out.
He killed Apsu, who foolishly sought to stand in
     his way,
seeking to protect Tiamat.
Cruelly she had sent him out to face the world-
     ruling hero,
and Marduk slew him, quickly and easily.
It was no great work for the Great One;
a little thing, like brushing aside an insect that
     sought to bite him.
Then, with her hero gone (could he really be called
     a hero? Marduk showed what a hero really was.),

Tiamat herself came against Marduk,
putting herself at risk.
Stretching wide her mouth, he killed her too.
The one who had cast dark fear on the hearts of the
     gods
died under the flashing power of Marduk.
He made short work of her, the Great Champion.
He split her wide open and formed from her earth
     and sky, and all between it.
He formed land and water, and men to serve the
     gods.
From emptiness, he formed presence,
from Chaos, there rose Cosmos under his extended
     hand.
The gods, seeing his complete victory over she
     whom they had feared,
gladly put into his keeping the lordship over all,
over gods and men.
They made him willingly, with gratitude for the
     great deed he had done,
the great king, to rule forever.
Those who know this,
those people, those lands,
that recognize his power,
are given his protection and blessings.
His mace is withheld from them,
and turned instead against their enemies.

That is why we turn with confidence to Marduk.
We have poured out beer to the Great Champion,
dutifully worshipped him,
and he will place his hand over us.
Marduk! King! Champion! Warrior! Hero!
If our words today have pleased you
If the offered beer has enflamed your heart
Remember us.
May our names not pass from your mind.
When you distribute blessings, hold us in your
    thoughts.
When you seek to punish, though,
when your mace urges you to cast it,
then forget us.
May we be hidden from your sight and from your
    memory.
Or, if you remember us,
may it be only to strike our enemies.
Marduk,
we have been loyal servants to you:
Be a good king over us.

★ I praise Marduk, mighty in battle,
who slew menacing Chaos,
yes, even Tiamat of the gaping jaws,
and her lover Apsu, when they rose against the gods.
Surely no disorder can withstand him,

surely not the small ones of my day.
A faithful servant to a well-disposed and powerful
  king,
I ask for this deserved reward.

*Meadow Spirits, with an offering of jewelry:*

★ I'm told you like pretty things, Meadow Spirits.

*Mithra:*

★ Great friend,
Lord of contracts,
Mithra of wide pastures:
my offering today is like a hand stretched out to you
  in friendship.

*Mother Earth:*

★ We return a portion of the earth's blessings.
May she continue to grant them,
and may we continue to deserve them.

*Perkʷúnos:*

★ Perkʷúnos, whose serpent-slaying
is world-creating,
is world-redeeming,
be with me in this day's rituals.

*Poseidon:*

★ Earthquake-bringer, destroyer of cities,
whose horse's hooves shatter the shores on which
  they land,
bring down the walls that surround me,

powder to dust their supporting stones,
view with the derision fit for a god their flaunted
    strengths:
free me from even my most beloved prisons;
release me to the widely extending world that
    awaits liberated souls.

*Raven:*

★ When I hear the clacking of your beak, the rough
    laughter from your throat,
I hope, Black-shrouded Flyer, that the joke isn't on me.

★ Okay, Raven, it was you, wasn't it, who [kept my car
    from starting, tripped me, rained on my parade,
    etc.]?
Me, I don't get the joke.
Laugh if you want to, but take this salmon and don't
    do it again.

*Rhiannon:*

★ It's quite obvious, really,
but at the same time a marvel:
a woman on a pale horse,
a woman who cannot be reached by great exertion.
Impossible to reach, she is easy to attain.
We need only call and ask for her love.
So I call to you, Rhiannon;
out of my need, I call to you.
I call to her—look, she stops.

Listen to my needs, Rhiannon,
fulfill them:
Please listen to someone who loves you.

*River Spirits:*

★ The spirit of this river is a snake winding through the
     land,
   its breath rising.
   I feed you with this; feed the land.

*Rock Spirits:*

★ What being, what spirit, has come to me in the
     shape of this stone?
   Or is it the rock itself to which I pour this out?
   I pour to the numinous before me.

*Sucellus, against limitations:*

★ Break the wall with your hammer, shake it to pieces,
     to thousands of pieces;
   reduce to sherds obstructing walls, Sucellus,
   between what I am and what I should be.
   Remove limitations, Mallet God,
   and open the possible.
   It only takes a tap from your irresistible force.

*Unknown deities:*

★ Whatever deity or spirit or ancestor
   whose presence I feel in this place:
   take this offering as a gift in return for your
     blessing.

★  These trees are the pillars,
   the roof the intertwining branches,
   with the scent of leaves and needles underfoot rising
        as incense.
   To which god or gods is this temple built?
   I don't know.
   I place this offering, then,
   and pour this libation,
   to the unknown divine present here
   and to the spirits of this place.

*Varuṇa, for fair play:*

★  Lord of Order, Varuṇa, of the Ṛta,
   Enforcer of the Sacred Law,
   whose snares await those who violate your
        Ordinances:
   inspire in me devotion to the rules of the game I am
        about to play.
   If my acts are not fair, they can never be excellent,
   and instead of glory will bring down on me your
        deserved punishment.

*Varuṇa, for right action:*

★  From the noose that ensnares those who violate
        the Ṛta,
   protect me, Varuṇa.
   From the noose that ensnares those who live by
        untruth,

protect me, Varuṇa.
From the noose that ensnares those to whom their
    Dharma is nothing,
protect me, O Varuṇa.

*Vedic deities, for friendship:*

★ Difficult as it may be for me to make friends,
teach me, Vāc, the words to say in this social
    situation.
Connect me, Aśvins, to others closely,
you who are connected closely to each other,
whose horses' gait brings people together.
Mitra, whose name is "friend,"
may I be seen as a friend to those I will meet.

*Wind:*

★ Carry in blessings,
giving wind.
Carry away ills,
cleansing wind.
Bring all that is good.
Remove all that is bad.
Leave me behind, happy and healthy.

*Zeus:*

★ If ever I have poured out libations to you,
or crumbled honey cakes in your honey,
accept this offering to you now
and look kindly on me.

# CHAPTER 15

# PROSPERITY

If the world is a sacred one, it follows that asking for things that will help us in this world is no bad thing. It is not defiling the sacred to want to have good things in life. Remember that the divine beings are entwined in the world of nature.

★ The rain will fall just like this [mead, beer, milk, etc.; depending on the deity addressed]
   if you like my offering.

*The All-Gods:*

★ Health and wealth, Keepers of Treasure, give your worshipper.
   May this little offering be returned a thousandfold.
   May my blessings be countless,
   scattered out from your storehouse with sweet-scented hands.

*Artemis, for a hunter:*

★ Knowing how much you value your modesty
   I'm not looking to find you as you go through these woods,
   Apollo's sister.
   But if you could send me a deer or two I would be very grateful,
   lovely Artemis.

*Ceres, for crops:*

★ Increase our crops.
Cause to increase our crops.
Bring rain and sun to increase our crops.
May your earth be fertile to increase our crops.
May your earth be fertile to cause to increase our
    crops.
Mother Ceres, may our crops increase.

*Commerce, for financial prosperity:*

★ Commerce, who links people together,
forming from them a community,
and then forming from communities a greater one—
from many one—
for the enrichment of all:
Respond to my prayer by enriching *me*,
I who take part in your communities.

*Earth, for food:*

★ Mother of earth and people and plants,
bring grain and milk for these children.

★ Dark and warm and strongly-scented,
shaping the seeds and roots of all living things,
be firm beneath my body, which lies on you,
and honor my faith by filling me with exactly what
    I need:
I won't ask you for more than that.

*G<sup>w</sup>ouwindā:*

★ From your heavenly udders,
round as the earth,
white as the moon,
pour out inexhaustible milk for your children who
    stand here with upraised hands.
We have offered to you, G<sup>w</sup>ouwindā,
you know we have,
and now we wait expectantly for you loving gifts,
Provider of Cows.

*Herakles, for help in difficulties:*

★ With arrows, you killed the snake of the Hesperides,
With a torch, the Hydra,
With your own hands, the Nemean lion.
I don't care what weapon you use as long as my dif-
    ficulties fall before you.

*Horus, against enemies:*

★ Falcon-headed, tear at their eyes.
Burning-orbed, wear them down.
Lord of North and South, strike them with your twin
    scepters.
This prayer is for Horus:
may he hear it.
Soarer, Shiner, Striker:
Destroy my enemies,
confound their plans,

bring me to victory,
that next time I burn incense to you, I will be one
victorious.

*Janus, when beginning something:*

★ I'm beginning something
so I'm looking to Janus with hope,
and pouring him this wine.

★ Janus is the blesser of the opening door.
Janus is the blesser of the setting forth.
Janus is the blesser of the arriving safely.
Janus is the blesser of the closing door.
As the god of beginnings he has, from the begin-
ning, blessed our beginnings,
As the god of endings he has, to the ending, blessed
our endings,
I can confidently pray to you, Janus Pater,
to hear my praise and petition.

*Kami, for the removal of obstacles:*

★ May the Kami of this [tool/weapon] shine [its/her/
is] power,
like that of a lightning flash in the black,
like that of a fire in a fireplace,
like that of the sun from rising to noon,
showing the way through difficulties,
smoothing the path between me and my goal,
shoving aside all the obstacles between me and
my path.

*Kwan Yin:*

★ On your lotus-petal way,
   strewn by your gentle hands,
   Kwan Yin, may I travel throughout my life.

*Mars:*

★ This ram, Father Mars, to you,
   that you may be increased in power
   that I may be increased in power
   for prosperity and protection.

*The Maruts, for rain:*

★ What is the clattering noise I hear, as tree limbs
      against each other?
   It is the Maruts, coming in splendor, bringing rain.
   What is the glittering fire I see, as of clouds hiding
      lightning?
   It is the Maruts, coming in splendor, bringing rain.
   What is the awe-inspiring presence I feel, as of the
      clashing of armies?
   It is the Maruts, coming in splendor, bringing rain.
   Splendorous Maruts, come quickly, bringing rain.

*Pūṣan:*

★ Glowing Pūṣan, who conveys the bride
   as if in your goat-guided chariot,
   to a peaceful life,
   bring me, as if wedded,
   to prosperity,
   lord of paths, deliverer.

*Storm God, for rain:*

★ Rain, God of Storms, send rain.
Not the lightning that obliterates everything it hits,
and not torrents that wash away the dirt from our
    plants and our homes,
but rain that falls gently,
lovingly even,
soaking into the ground where it can be used by
    living beings.
Rain, Storm God, send rain.

★ The rest of my neighborhood is soaking their lawns
    each day with water from distant lakes,
but I am waiting for rain.
Grass at this time of the year is *supposed* to be
    brown and brittle; I know that.
But grass is so beautiful when it is green and soft.
So I'm waiting patiently for you to return:
but hurry.

★ On the heads of my enemies drop your axe,
a thunderbolt from a clear sky.

*Thunderbird, for rain:*

★ Lightning in dry air over the burnt land, hey!
Fire in the dry air over the burnt land, hey!
Rain clouds in the dry air over the burnt land, hey!
Thunderbird, trailing fire in his wings, comes.

Thunderbird, carrying roars in their beating, comes.
Thunderbird, bringing rain to the burnt land, comes.
Thunderbird, we will turn wet faces to you, hey,
when you pass over us.

★ May the roaring flapping of your wings be the
    thunder accompanying the storm.
May the cutting flashing of your eyes be the light-
    ning accompanying the story.
May the rhythmic clacking of your beak be the rain's
    music as it falls, be the storm,
which will come as you fly to us,
as you fly, Storm-Bringing Thunderbird.

*Spirits of Prey, for a hunter:*

★ [animal's name], I have a deal for you:
come to my gun and I will honor and remember you.

## Work

*Earth and Water Spirits:*

★ Through long time fine soil has been laid down by
water to make the clay with which I form this vessel.
Every liquid poured into or from it will be a libation
    to earth and water.

*Hephaestus:*

★ Though crippled, you possess great skill in
    compensation.

Hephaestus, of power and skill, show sympathy for
    my own shortcomings
and guide me, and aid me, to produce works with
    quality.

*Lugh:*

★  Lugh, of arts and skills,
as your spear,
so my hammer:
May it fall powerfully and accurately,
and may my work be performed with beauty and
    without delay.

*Vulcan:*

★  When the gods want the best,
in strength or art,
they turn to you, Vulcan.
And so do I:
not for you to do the work,
but to guide my arms.
Although my work can't equal yours,
may it be the best possible for mortal man.

★  The strong arms that drive the hammer against the
    metal on the anvil,
causing the crash that deafens my ears among the
    liquid flames of the volcano where your smithy
    is hidden,

end in clever fingers, which create fine work to
cause as much marvel for their artistry as your
rougher work for its utility.

Guide my work, both rough and fine, Vulcan, and the
praise I receive from others will be praise of you.

# CHAPTER 16

# THOUGHT, SPEECH, INSPIRATION

There is more to existence than the material. Humans are thinking animals, and so by thinking better, we become more human, more what we are. To ask divine help for thought is to ask for help in being natural, which is certainly something that would interest the sacred beings of nature.

We are also animals who speak and in the same way, speaking well is being good at being a human. Both thought and speech overlap with inspiration, which helps us think new thoughts and speak beautiful words.

The divine beings like pretty words. So as well as wanting us to be what we are, they also want to hear nice things from us. Callings, praise, thanks, and all the other purposes of prayer come across more nicely if we are inspired.

Inspiration and speech also help us be more aware of the world—both sacred and mundane. Through them, we are therefore put more in touch with all that is.

★ When I speak, may my words be as clear to my
    listeners as you would be to me, if I only knew
    how to listen.

★ Speak my words,
  comes the god's hidden voice.
  When I open my mouth, may this be true.

*Agni, to assist in prayers:*

★  If your tongues will speak my words
   I will feed you with butter;
   and you will grow strong and carry my prayers to
        the gods.

*The All-Gods, for patience:*

★  Piece, by piece, by piece, fills the pot.
   Step, by step, by step, finds the goal.
   One, plus one, plus one, and the infinite sum is
        attained.
   Patience, Old Ones, Patience:
   You know how to wait with patience.
   I ask for patience that I may wait.
   May I wait in patience.

★  Yes, but.
   No, but.
   When I form opinions may I always remember "but,"
   because, All-Gods, that is often where truth is found.

*Apollo, for thinking well:*

★  Each word you speak a song.
   each line a symphony:
   so too today, my speech,
   Son of Leto.
   Give me a clear mind to receive your wisdom,
   and a mind filled with the skill to use it once given.

*Apollo, for true thought:*

★ Remove from my mind all illusion, Far-Seeing Apollo.
Light me a path through confusion, Ordering Apollo.
For true is the speech from you to each who ask for
    your help, Apollo.

*Apollo, for truth:*

★ Far-seer:
May I know logos.
May I speak logos.
May I *be* logos.
Truth is what I ask of you.
If I have satisfied,
send Truth.

*Apollo, for musical skill:*

★ A true song is one inspired by the god of truth and
    music,
whose lyre shines like the lucent sun.
May the song I am writing be a true one, Apollo,
and in its singing all will know of your matchless
    perfection.

★ Player on the lyre,
fill my fingers as they [strum, pluck, bow]
the strings of my [instrument].

*Apollo, for inspiration in speech:*

★ Apollo, inspirer of all who speak,
may each word I say today be like an arrow into the
    minds of my listeners,

as if launched from your never-erring bow,
and inform, educate, and persuade them.

*Apollo and Hermes, for help for a scientist:*

★ Apollo, Lord of Truth, may I see into the truth when
     I perform my research today.
Apollo, Lord of the Good, may I create beautiful
     theories from it.
Hermes, god of trickery and speech, may I see
     beyond the obvious, no matter how attractive,
and convey it to others in attractive words,
although under your friend Apollo's watchful eye;
may the attractive be True, may the True be the Good.

*Athena, for help in using skills:*

★ Knowledge alone will not suffice:
with wisdom to use it, bless my mind,
Athena, whose skillful touch is sure to those who
     worship you,
with well-wrought words,
with well-crafted deeds.

*Athena or Minerva, for inspiration:*

★ With one small reflection of the mind of creation
     whose home is in your helmeted head,
gift me, Maiden, as I set about this creation of
     my own.

*Aushrine, for inspired speech:*

★ As the many colors of your miracle rainbow
     extending from earth to heaven,

so too may my words be here today.
Aushrine, who brings the shining sun,
bring the Shining Ones to hear my words,
and may my words, through you, shine to please
    them.

*Brighid, for fair speech:*

★ Make my words sweet enough to call you here,
and sweet enough to praise you when you arrive,
Sweet Brighid.

*Brighid, for inspired speech:*

★ May Brighid place her fire in my head,
her liquid flame flowing from my mouth,
burning with truth.

*Cernunnos, for making a decision:*

★ May I see both sides,
weighing them fairly before striking out with a deci-
    sion, Cernunnos,
drawing my strength from the tension and peace of
    the middle,
just as you do, Cernunnos:
the power you wield in the service of our purposes
comes from the purity of its time and intent.
Make me more like that, Cernunnos.

*Cernunnos, for wisdom:*

★ Wisdom is found in-between, where the view is best.
Lord of the in-between, lead me to wisdom.

*Computer Spirit, for inspired writing:*

★   As the electrons travel my neurons,
    so too in this computer.
    As my thoughts are divine,
    so too with this computer.
    May we write well together,
    spirit with spirit.

*Crossing into the sacred:*

★   A deer knows the ways of the forest's edge,
    and you who wear a crown of antlers
    know the way between our world and the wild.
    May I cross the border between all worlds
    safely, with you beside me, Lord.

*Dawn, for inspired speech:*

★   Any time is yours, young Lady, whose entrance
        announces with wordless prayer a new light.
    Dawn within me now; with words as sweet as your
        morning song, awaken in me my own voice,
    let it rise to your ears, let it rise to the ears of the
        Holy Ones,
    let it rise as your sweet mead that flames on the
        morning horizon.
    Any time is yours, welcome child:
    may this be a time for you to dawn in me.

★   Just as you rise in the East, Maiden of Dawn,
    raise in me poetry;

just as you bring the sun,
bring from me dazzling words.

*Dawn, for inspiration:*

★ For us who wander blindly,
in ignorance or despair,
blossom in the darkness,
your rose petals pushing back the night,
as you rise in our hearts.

*Dionysos, for performance inspiration:*

★ I wait in the dark for the curtain to rise,
for Dionysos to arrive.
Bring music and dance, ecstatic god.

*Fire or Fire Deity, for truth:*

★ Fire's teeth cut.
Fire's heat burns.
Fire's light shines.
Fire's tongue teaches.
Fire, help me decide the truth.

*Gaṇeśa, for patience:*

★ Patient as your ponderous feet,
make me, Gaṇeśa.

*The God:*

★ God of transformation, reach into me for a piece of
treasure I am best without.
Accept this beloved fault as an appropriate offering,

presenting me in return with the perfect gift of your
    gift's removal:
precious gain from precious loss,
Transforming God.

*The Goddess:*

★ "Listen," she says, "just listen:
Still the rambling thoughts,
quiet the restless mind,
stem the stream of words,
and listen for a moment.
Just a moment is all I ask,
is all I need, for you to hear me,
just one.
"Listen," she says.
Speak, and I will listen.

*The Goddess, for advice:*

★ As Maiden of the waxing moon, enliven my mind.
As Mother of the full, give maternal guidance.
As Crone who brings the dwindling light, bring final
    wisdom.
Under whatever phase, in whatever guise,
you who are the constant moon,
teach this child of yours this moment's is and ought.

*Hekate, for wisdom:*

★ Your torch has brought me here.
Your knife bars the path.

Burn, cut away,
Wisdom-bringer.

*Helios, for self-transformation:*

★ You, Helios, see everything through your light that
    shines on us.
I open myself to that light;
I welcome you to my most inner places,
to shine in my darkness.
Each hidden secret,
each unknown shame,
each unrecognized flaw,
all that is in me that I have pushed deep away,
and denied the existence of my responsibility for:
fill these with your unrelenting scrutinizing fire,
show them to me with irresistible clarity.
And when I run from these terrors, leave me no
    place to hide.
When I seem to rationalize, leave me no
    explanation,
and when I seek to excuse them, leave me nothing
    on which to base my excuses.
And when I submit myself at last to the truth you
    display,
may it be a purifying river of molten gold into which
    I am thrown.
I will burn:
but oh, how I'll shine!

*Indra, for inspiration:*

★  Indra having stolen, as an eagle,
   the sacred drink, the soma,
   from the Asuras,
   the snakes who raise themselves against the gods,
   became strong.
   I, in drinking these Waters of Life,
   derive for myself not only strength,
   but inspired sight.

*Jupiter, for decision:*

★  Sceptered, enthroned,
   with eagle crowned,
   you rule, greatest Jupiter, over the cosmos.
   May my actions be such as will win your approval.
   Guide me, Father, in my decisions.

*Lugh, for confidence:*

★  Fear is cut through
   by the spear of Lugh.

*Manannán mac Lir, against regret:*

★  With a swift shake of your cloak, Manannán,
   separate my thoughts from regretted memories,
   leaving only a not-understood gratitude.

*Manannán mac Lir, for clear thought:*

★  Fog-ridden is my bedeviled mind,
   mist-filled my thoughts.
   If it be the shaking of your cloak, son of the sea,

shake it again, banishing the mist,
clearing the cloud-covered sky to show me the guid-
    ing star
that shines from your divine brow.

*Mars, for social courage:*

★  May fear and shyness that blocks the bridges I try to
        build to others
be themselves blocked from entering my mind, Mars,
you who bind people to others and protect the
        peace of society.

*Menot, for clear thought:*

★  Measuring is true.
If measuring is true, it must fit.
Does this fit?
It doesn't.
Menot, may my mind fit.

*Menot, for memory:*

★  Menot, make me remember the unremembered.

*Menot, for knowledge:*

★  Measuring time,
Measuring space,
Measuring well,
you always find the right answer.
No surprise that, since the answer only exists
        because of the measuring,
as that made by your ever-turning wheel

that rolls through the night sky.
True measurement brings light to the darkness.
True worship of you, Menot,
opens our minds and dispels ignorance.

*Menot, for clear thought:*

★ Though ecstatic utterances gush freely from the well
    that burns,
unless cooled by your ordering they are mad
    jabberings.
No matter where I find my words, I turn to Menot to
    help me shape them,
to form a song of beauty from them,
inspired, but well put,
measured out to fit.

*Moon, for true thought:*

★ Moon, who measures out time and space,
who puts this here, and that there,
this then, the other in its own time,
who orders that which is as it should be:
teach me to divide properly all I experience;
teach me to divine all I need to know,
that my life may be true,
that I may live in the Truth.

*Moon, against bad thoughts:*

★ The confusion in my mind,
Measurer of the Sky, of Time:

bring order to it.
You divide the unmeasured,
and put each thing in its proper place:
do that as well with my suffering-causing thoughts:
Heal my soul.

*Nature Spirits, for understanding nature:*

★ When nature speaks to me, may I hear.
May I know the language of birds and animals.
May I understand the sounds of swaying grass and
   the creaking of tree limbs.
May I perceive the tiny sounds of stones as well as
   the roarings, the murmurings of water.
May I come to know the music of the spheres sung
   in the empty space between the celestial bodies.
May I hear in them the epics they have been telling
   each other since the beginning of time.

*Odin, for poetic inspiration:*

★ Even if you have to use deceit to break through my
   armored walls to find there the inspiring drink
   my outward-facing eyes had never known was
   there, gray-cloaked wanderer, your face only
   half-hidden by your drooping hat, befuddle my
   mind so I don't remember the tales well enough
   to recognize you; slip through before I can put
   up my fearful senses.
I want you to bring the drink of poetry to me to
   swallow, but knowing the stories of what your

own wisdom cost you, I think I'm quite justified
in being afraid of what you'll want from me.

I'll look aside, then, avert my gaze, and you can
sneak up on me, and rip out the hidden poetic
madness in one quick motion, and then hold it
out to me as if it were not your eye-payment,
but mine instead.

Show me my unknown talents for inspiration, Odin,
and I will know what else I need, and so be willing to pay the cost, even if it be as great as that
you paid without hesitation.

*Oghma, for clear writing:*

★ Deviser of alphabets,
be an unobstructing conduit of ideas between me
and my readers,
Oghma, through whose gifts speech becomes seen.

*Pan, for musicians:*

★ Pan, be in their drums,
Pan, be in their guitars,
Pan, be in their basses,
Pan, be in their bodies and voices,
those of the band about to perform.

*Sarasvati, for true speech:*

★ A sweet river, as of milk,
Sarasvati, with amṛta in her hands,
gives gifts, protects, inspires.

She is worthy of praise,
beautiful in her arising:
My prayer to her for true words.

*Sarasvati, for inspired speech:*

★ White river, poured-out stream,
Sarasvati, carry words from the divine lands to my
        lips;
may the sacred find its way into my speech, my
        prayers,
may the gods be called in words they themselves
        have inspired.

*Sarasvati, for musical inspiration:*

★ Sarasvati's strings be found in my voice,
stream through my fingers,
vibrate in my heart.

*A Sky God, against anger:*

★ Anger brings confusion.
Make my mind as clear as your most cloudless sky:
God the Firmament.

*Silence:*

★ I would pray to Silence,
but I won't.

*Speech:*

· ★ Semantics of all words,
Syntax of all sentences,
Former of utterances:

Speech, may all I say express perfectly my will,
and that of the Holy Ones,
binding us together in one speech-community.

*Sun, against confusion:*

★ You whose rays cross the empty spaces,
bringing light to the darkened land,
revealing the night-concealed:
cut through, O Sun, the fog of my mind,
the mist that stands between me and the truth.
Remove, Light-Giver, Way-Shower,
the blinds that keep me from knowing things as
    they really are.

*Tahuti, for understanding while reading:*

★ Ibis-headed one, Tahuti,
may I read this book with a bird's clear sight,
Weigher of Words.

*Thoth, for understanding while reading:*

★ When I open this book, open my mind, Thoth,
let the thoughts in.
But as the thoughts enter, Thoth,
inspire my discrimination;
may I consider but not be manipulated by these
    ideas.

*Vāc, for inspired speech:*

★ Vāc gives me the words to praise here,
words given by Word,

but leaving some to join myself with other people,
and to praise other gods.
I thank her for the joining and praise,
hoping it will continue,
her words pouring into me to pour out again.
And I have to wonder whether the gods thank her as
    well for providing the means to praise them.
Gods, let's join together to praise her.

★   Each new word I learn a new thought,
    a new way to praise Vāc.
    Help me, speech.

*Vāc, for simple speech:*

★   I speak to Word with the simplest words I know,
    for simpler words,
    for words more true.

*Vāc, for inspired writing:*

★   Sitting in front of my computer's screen,
    my fingers prepared to strike the keys,
    I pause a moment to ask inspiration
    by you, O Vāc: may my words flow freely.

*Venus, for giving love:*

★   Show me, Venus, the way to show my love to those
        whom I love that they may know.

*Winds:*

★   May words be blown my way, carried on the winds
        by the gods of the winds,

to issue forth again, woven into beautiful patterns,
as hymns, as prayers, carried on the breath.

*Woden, for guidance:*

★  All who wander without direction:
to these, Woden, be a guide.
All who puzzle without solution:
to these, Woden, be a guide.
All who search without finding:
to these, Woden, be a guide.
All who inquire without answer:
to these, Woden, be a guide.
All who seek without obtaining:
to these, Woden, be a guide.
God who understands:
to those to whom the journey is worth the cost,
even not arriving,
to these, Woden, be a guide.

*Writing God, for inspired writing:*

★  You whose fingers hold the pen,
or stroke the keys,
whose output of words flows continuously,
and never ceases,
and never ceases to amaze:
God of Writing, inspire me as I begin to write,
be my model.

*Xáryomen, for clear thought:*

★ Knit together the fragments of my tattered mind,
that spread, Xáryomen, through my life,
into one complete cloth,
beautiful, whole,
and ready to be shaped.

*Zeus, for clear thought:*

★ As clear as your cloudless sky,
my mind, Zeus, my mind.

## Divination

★ I [choose these runes/place these cards/cast these
coins, etc.] to know what is, and, from that,
what will be.
May this small thing be a true reflection of the great
thing,
so that, by understanding this, I might understand
that.
God(s)/Goddess(es) of prophecy [or their names],
may I read correctly what I am shown.
I ask your help in seeing only what is true,
not just what I want to see.

★ Spirits of these tools of divination, my question is
this:
[Question]
Answer, and I will listen.

★   May the deity of this moment guide my reaching
        fingers toward the true divination tokens.

★   In the next words I hear,
    speak wisdom, speak truth,
    make clear the path that lies before me,
    that in the days to come I must walk.
    May the words of strangers not be idle talk,
    but words from the source.

*The Goddess:*

★   The World, which speaks,
    the Goddess, whose words they are,
    whose body is the world,
    is the Earth who gives our own bodies their birth,
    is speaking to us in words that seem mad:
    mad words of a mad priestess,
    as the cryptic utterances of the Python of Delphi,
    sitting on the tripod over the cleft,
    breathing the fumes, tasting the laurel she chewed.
    Mad words of uncertain meaning,
    difficult to interpret,
    dangerous to follow,
    but even more to ignore,
    and always true.
    These are the words, the type of words, the World
        speaks,
    the utterances of the Goddess;

these are the words we must listen for,
and listen to,
though they come to us half-heard,
hints from the edge of sound and sanity,
blown to our ears on the fluttering wind.
Though obscure, though the seeming ravings of a
    disordered mind,
they are still Her words.
I doubt them:
in my doubt, may I listen.
I lack faith in them:
may they speak to my soul.
I do not trust them:
may I know them to be true.
May she speak with sure words
and may I listen with sure understanding,
or if I do not understand them,
with wonder, with amazement, with awe, with love,
may I still listen to the words she speaks.

*Odin:*

★  Speak to me, Odin, through the casting of the runes,
   and I will listen.

★  Odin, who speaks in riddles and hints,
   speak clearly through the runes I draw.

# CHAPTER 17

# HEALING, COMFORT, SAFETY, TRAVEL

Healing, comfort, safety, and protection for travelers were very common goals of prayer in ancient times. We have many offerings made for healing (and in gratitude for it), as well as entire temples dedicated to healing deities. There are also deities of travel to ask for easy passage and safe return, and there are prayers preserved to local beings— river spirits, for instance, who are asked for a safe crossing.

Comfort is a major function of religion. The deities tell us that there is more beyond our everyday lives and, as our friends, they want us to feel better. Parental deities want to act as parents would, and many others want to stand with us in our needs. That's what friends do, and the goal of many of the other prayers in this book is to make friends with the gods.

★ For every person,
  for each one, single,
  of unfathomed worth,
  who cries at night from hunger,
  from fear,
  from soul-eating loneliness;

for each and for all who suffer amidst rejoicing,
or starve amongst plenty,
or stand alone while others live with families and
    friends about them:
Today, I am praying for them.
You Gods, each and several of every power and
    disposition,
I place these people into your care.

## Healing

★ Just as this strengthens you,
    strengthen my immune system against this disease.

★ Healing gods, guide the hands and minds and
        caring hearts
    of nurses and doctors upon whose healing skills I
        depend.

*The All-Gods:*

★ The All-Gods expel this illness from you,
    disease, and pain, and tiredness, and suffering,
    ill-health, and depression, and body aches.
    These seek to destroy the order of life.
    The All-Gods despise disorder and will defeat them.
    You can be sure of this:
    it is their way.

*Airmed:*

★ From her grave grew herbs of great power,
Airmed, daughter of Diancecht.
This herb is of great power,
Airmed, daughter of Diancecht.
May it heal me with part of your great power,
Airmed, daughter of Diancecht.

★ Airmed, from whose broken body healing herbs
    grew,
may this medicine be like them.
May your future praise come from a healthy
    worshipper.

*Apollo:*

★ Flights of arrows descend from your ever-
    turning bow,
onto those who look toward you from below.
Flights of arrows that bring disease or healing
onto those who look toward you from below.
We who look toward you ask that they be causes of
    healing,
that their killing power be directed toward illness.
Do this and we will always have good reasons to
    praise you.

*Apollo, against cancer:*

★ Apollo, God of the Logos,
of the Truth that is behind the form,

whose lyre sings forth harmony.
God of the pattern that is,
and thus of the shape that should be:
you are rightly called Great Healer,
returning life to its proper place,
setting it firmly within the natural Order of things.
Rain down your unfailing arrows on this illness;
pierce the crab's hard shell,
cut it cleanly about its edges,
drive straight through its heart and carry it away,
leaving a purified body behind.
I have always revered the Logos, Son of Leto,
and dedicated myself to it.
You know that, God of the Bow,
so when I pour out this libation in your honor
I know you will look kindly on me and answer my
    prayer.

★ Woken in the night by a pain in my stomach
I pray to you for cease of its prodding
and a return to healing sleep,
Apollo of the shining bow.

*Apollo or Brighid:*
★ With your vivifying flame fill with vitality this loved
    one who lies here ailing,
Bright One who heals.

*Asklepios:*

★ It was an honor for you to be struck down by the
        hand of Zeus,
    a great honor to be so treated,
    the greatest of honors to be so feared by the gods.
    You were breaking the natural order of things, keep-
        ing men from death,
    so you were punished.
    Zeus treated you justly, Asklepios,
    and I have no quarrel with him.
    I don't ask for immortality, then,
    but only for health in the time allotted me.
    The gods may know what that time is
    (or maybe they don't; maybe it is in the hands of a
        Fate beyond them)
    but I do not.
    So I ask you, Asklepios, for health while I live.
    End this sickness that weighs me down.
    You have the power and need only use it.
    Give health to one who confidently worships you.

★ As I touch this patient,
    may my fingers be each like your staff, Asklepios.
    As I speak this prayer, giver of true diagnoses,
    may my words be like the lapping of the gentle
        snakes that surround it.
    May everything I do to heal [name] be exactly what
        you would have done if you were the doctor here.

*Brighid:*

★ Brighid who guides a healer's hands,
whose fire inspires soothing words,
be with me as I greet this patient:
may diagnosis and treatment be true.

★ The hammer on the anvil
creates delicate beauty.
The fire in the forge
creates delicate beauty.
May the force and fire within which I live
create delicate beauty,
beautiful Brighid.

*Death:*

★ If I give this to you, Death, will you go?
Will you return on your well-marked path to the
        enclosed place?
Will you stay far away for many years left unlived?
Will it be a payment for your time waiting?
Take this, then, and go.

★ You have your own place, Death,
and this is not it.
There you rule as king;
here we are the most common of people.
There you dwell in a noble palace;
here we live in a simple house.

There you enjoy sparkling riches;
here our poverty shames us.
Go to your place, Death,
and wait for us there.
We have heard your message and we will respond.
But we are busy here, Death.
We have many things to do.
Be patient, we will respond,
but only when the time is right.
Return to your home, Death,
and wait for us to come.
For you it will be only a little while.
For us, it will have been a lifetime.

*Firebird:*

★ Firebird, who dwells on the Tree of Life,
bring some of its fruit to me,
to heal my sickness,
to return me to health,
and I will praise you.

*The Goddess:*

★ Mother of all that lives
and all that dies,
promote life,
defeat illness and death,
in this one who comes to you with love.

*Kwan Yin, for someone with Alzheimer's:*

★ As my [loved one/father/mother, etc.] descends into
      the fog of Alzheimer's,
   Kwan Yin of the beatific smile,
   with each moment draw [him/her] closer in the
      strong and gentle hug of your encircling arms.
   In this troubling time, may [he/she] find your peace.

*Mithras:*

★ Mithras Soter,
   Mithras Pater,
   Mithras of the Ever-Descending Knife:
   Through your obedience to Sol Invictus
   you rose to be with him,
   to grasp hands with him,
   to feast with him.
   May I be as obedient to you.
   May you alone be my crown.
   May I come to sit beside you in the never-ending
      feast,
   there among the stars.
   Through Mercury, may I rise.
   Through Venus, may I rise.
   Through Mars, may I rise.
   Through Jupiter, may I rise.
   Through the Moon, may I rise.
   Through the Sun, may I rise.
   Through Saturn may I rise.

Through the agency of the salvific bull-slaying,
May I rise,
May I be made immortal.

*Moon:*

★ We pray for light's power to heal this person.
Not *your* light, though, Sun.
The fierce purity of your blazing would harm more
    than heal.
Another time we will come to you with respect and
    offerings.
Tonight, we turn to Luna of the soft light.
With this bowl of milk, we ask you to pour your own
    healing swiftness over this one.
Swathe [her/him] in your sweet unguent;
with it draw anything inimical to health out from
    [her/his] body.
You are dependable in your constant turning
so we feel confident to depend on you for this.

## Comfort

★ I place myself in the center of the turning world:
the center is still.

★ Maybe I have as many troubles as there are grains of
    sand on all the beaches of the world.
But there are more of you than all the grains of sand
    on all the beaches of all the worlds in all the
    universes.

With your irresistible power you can crush them into
    powder and wash them away if you want.
Please want to.

*The All-Gods:*

★  All-Gods,
    each god,
    joined together in perfect relationships:
    I hunger for friends to fill my lonely days,
    and it is to you whom I turn for help.
    Bring me in contact with the right people
    and advise me on how to do the rest.

*Cernunnos:*

★  I saw him.
    I saw Cernunnos in the eye of the whirlwind.
    I saw the one with antlers sitting in the axle of the
        midst of the world's turning.
    He was the very force of calm force;
    still, but ready to lash out in any direction;
    balanced on the cusp, the nexus between one
        moment and the next.
    I saw him
    and this is what he told me to tell you:
    be at peace.

★  You with the antlers,
    It is always still where you sit in the center of the
        whirling storm.

When the winds whirl about me,
be the rock to which I cling.
I pray, Lord Cernunnos, for a share of your peace.

★ Calm, still Lord, may I be calm.

*Dawn:*

★ It matters not that the sun shines on those
    around me,
or even if it's highest on the brightest day of the
    year,
I am still in darkness, my soul open and aching.
I cry for the light, the truest light,
I cry for it to fill the hole within.
Dawn, open your gates in me, and bring the dawn
    to my soul,
unlock the gates of my heart,
and create a path where people might walk through
    open doors.

*The God:*

★ Old fierceness is what you show us,
fierceness no less strong because it's old.
For the age is not in your body, but in your eyes;
a little tired, perhaps, from having seen so much.
But like so many fathers the fierceness is love.
Fierceness isn't always motivated by cruelty;
a father's fierceness may be of respect,

not letting us win games by throwing them,
but making us beat them fairly,
thereby gaining our own respect to match theirs.
Sometimes it is silence, like fishing beside each
    other,
sometimes talking on a long road trip.
Men are often bad at putting things into words
but express their love no less through deeds,
even though that may be hard to see:
The man who carries the heaviest suitcase, even
    though he's sick too,
is speaking his love.
The husband and father who goes each day to
    health-destroying work,
is speaking his love.
If we don't see this, it's *our* fault, not his,
and although you are a god, you are purely a man,
    and show your love through deeds.
Not a soft love, but love so hard it sometimes
    doesn't seem as if it's there.
But the fault is *ours*.
So when I come to you, looking for comfort,
I don't expect hugs, or soothing touches,
I expect comfort, sure, but the comfort comes in
    these words:
"OK; let's get to work fixing this—
we'll do it together."

And we will.

★ In [my/our/their] darkness give light,
   Lord of Brilliance.

★ Destroy all fear in me,
   Lord whose sharp-tined antlers carry all faults away,
   carry them in tatters.

*The Goddess:*

★ Her love is perfect, and perfectly She expresses it.
   Loving all, She gives all love,
   with Her, all things are done with Her love for all.
   And yet—
   and yet—
   and yet—
   I'm suffering.
   She loves all, but She doesn't love each.
   So many have died so I could live,
   unless I die, so many will never live.
   And yet—
   and yet—
   and yet—
   and yet, Greatest of Lovers,
   may this be my day.
   May Your love for me be Your love for all.
   May I see Your smile
   and smell Your sweet breath as you say:
   "Peace."

★ Mother, can you hear me crying?
  Gather me in your infinitely encompassing arms,
  hug me to your soft breast,
  and whisper, "There, There;
  all will be well.
  All will be well, but for now cry.
  My clothes have been wet with tears before and will
      be again.
  So for now, cry,
  and all will be well."

★ Inside the tadpole, the frog.
  Inside the caterpillar, the butterfly.
  Inside my pain, happiness.
  I don't doubt your ways, Goddess of Nature,
  nor do I want to criticize you,
  but they're hard.
  Send me strength and comfort, until I see what will
      come of the way things are.

★ Adrift in the unseen waves of the infinite dark I float
      at ease,
  resting trustingly in your enveloping arms.

★ I'm crying,
  lonely,
  my tears Your ocean's waters.

★ Not true, not true, not true, not true, not true,
        not true;
    it can't be true.
    All I want is for you to hold me and say, "Even if it's
        true, it will be OK."
    Please, Mother.
    Please.

★ Broken and tired and scared and scarred,
    I sit empty,
    and wait for Her to fill me,
    and wait for Her to dive deep into my emptiness,
    and return clutching my lost self tightly,
    and return it to me with smiling eyes,
    with soft hands open and soothing.

★ The Goddess sits beside me as I wait for your night
        terrors to subside.

★ Sitting here, looking at the moon, at the Lady whose
        changing is yet regular, assured, and reliable, I
        ask her to give meaning to the mess I'm in.
    Spinner of the Night, may the web I find myself in
        trap blessings.

★ If you have any fears, bring them to Her,
    to the Mother of All,
    She whose presence is soothing,
    whose hands hold love.

*Hathor:*

★ Our mother, Hathor:
bring us children.
Inexhaustible udders:
give them prosperity.
Ever-loving cow:
may your lowing be always the loving murmur of a
    soothing lullaby.

*Inanna:*

★ As you went in quest to rescue Dumuzi from the
    land of the dead,
from the hand of your sister,
from the hand of Erishkigal,
Inanna, Rescuer of the Despondent,
raise me from my depression,
from the darkness with which I am beset,
from the shadow which surrounds my soul.

*Isis:*

★ When Osiris was slain, and divided into pieces
    scattered over the land,
you went and found them one by one, recovering,
    Isis, the lost,
a wife's love driving you on.
Search out all I have lost to time and age and sorrow,
and return it to me, each bit, one by one,
with a mother's love.

*Nuit:*

★ Fearful things surround me and fear rises in me:
Absorb both fearing and feared into your all-
    containing body, Nuit,
and leave me free.

*Odin:*

★ Pierced and hanged, with bleeding eye,
inspire me in my suffering time
with hope for wisdom at its end.

*Peace:*

★ Come to me, Peace,
as you would to the world.
As you would calm strife,
calm my mind.
As you would banish weapons,
banish my self-doubt.
As you would bring happiness,
bring it to me.
Come, Peace, bring peace,
to me as you would to the world.

*Pearl Spirit:*

★ An irritated oyster gave birth to this pearl, which is
    so softly beautiful.
Pearl, produce soft beauty from the hardship of my
    life as I wear you.

*Perkʷúnos :*

★ My voice may not be as loud as yours,
but it comes from my essential being too.
May it rise through the crash of clouds and into your
     ears, Perkʷúnos,
you who obliterate all that stands in your way.
May I be filled with the booming brightness you hurl
     and not by my fears.
May my body tremble with the strength of your
     arms and not my weakness.
May all I do be with your unfailing accuracy and
     your power which cannot be withstood.

*Sun:*

★ Feeling the shadow creeping upon me from behind
I pray to the last of the light to sustain me through
     the darkness with the knowledge of your return.
Keep me in this awareness:
Dark follows light, as it must,
but it must as well surrender to light when the
     proper time comes.
Just as you, setting Sun, may I know the proper time
     to come out of my sorrow as that time arises.

*Wind:*

★ The wind that blows through empty human halls
is the wind that blows through the empty deserts
is the wind that blows through the emptiness of all
     empty spaces

is the wind that blows through my own empty time.
But if you blow, wind, then there can be no
    emptiness.
Blow in my heart and keep this lonely one company.

## Safety

*Ares:*

★ Spear against shield strikes fear in those arrayed
against me,
but not in me,
because you and I are brothers, Ares,
in arms and at the table.

*Athena or Minerva:*

★ Armored one, with the aegis on your breast:
to you, praise,
from you, protection.
The one deserved, the other hoped for.

*Castor and Pollux:*

★ On either side of my AFV ride,
sons of Zeus.
May my treads be as well-placed and unfaltering as
    the hooves of your own steeds.
May each piece of ordinance that flies from me be
    like your spears,
as sure in aim and as certain in destructive power.
Bring me through this battle successfully,

Dioskouri;

may my mission be fully accomplished.

Then, when you have brought me back to base
  unharmed,

I will offer to you in thanks.

This is my vow to you, Castor and Pollux.

★ Saviors at sea,

Sons of God,

Divine brothers:

Watch over this ship as it sails into danger.

Protect it and all who sail on it,

that we may return home safely to port when our
  mission is accomplished.

*The Elements:*

★ I put you in the hands of the ones whose realms are
  in the elements.

I put you in the hands of the Air Beings:

may they protect you when you enter their lands;

when you think, may you be safe and true.

I put you in the hands of the Fire Beings:

may they protect you when you enter their lands;

when you act, may you be safe and true.

I put you in the hands of the Water Beings:

may they protect you when you enter their lands;

when you feel, may you be safe and true.

I put you in the hands of the Earth Beings:

may they protect you when you enter their lands;
when you are still, may you be safe and true.
I put you in the hands of the Spirit Beings:
may they protect you when you enter their lands
when you are, when you do, when you are in the
　　　midst of all,
may you be safe and true.

★ If wind blows you away, you will be protected by Air.
If flames rise around you, you will be protected by
　　　Fire.
If waves overwhelm you, you will be protected by
　　　Water.
If gravity drags you down, you will be protected by
　　　Earth.
In all of these dangers, Spirit will never abandon you,
as you lie within the protection of the elements.

*Manannán mac Lir:*

★ Wheel wells not awash,
rims not even damp,
on a flowery plain a chariot comes to me here in my
　　　boat.
Amazement not even relevant, since gods perform
　　　miracles,
and you, Manannán, are most certainly a god.
If the waves on which I sail can never be flowers
　　　under my keel,

may they at least be your horses carrying me safely,
with still manes.

*Marduk:*

★　Marduk, whose mace is ever ready to crush the
　　　　enemies of those who worship you,
of your faithful servants,
of we who pour out this beer,
who lay out this bread,
before your image.
Destroyer of Tiamat,
Defender of cities:
Protect us,
protect those who offer to you today.

*Morrígain:*

★　A snake that is not a snake,
A dog that is not a dog,
A cow that is not a cow—
You are not these things, Morrígain,
and I am not sure I want to know what you *are*.
If my offering pleases you, though,
protect rather than destroy.

*Ocean:*

★　All life began in you;
preserve my life while I sail on you.

★　I draw myself under the seen,
entering your hidden water world.

I rise up to where your waves reach over me,
where sense meets the incomprehensible.
May this gift of honor to you inspire a gift in return:
may you keep me safe when I sail on your surface.

*Peace:*

★   Far from home,
    living with fear,
    I pray for Peace to pull all the world into Her
        embrace.

*Poseidon, against an earthquake:*

★   Still the earth beneath me
    and I will pour you a libation of wine,
    blue-maned hurler of the trident.

*Thor and Odin:*

★   Arriving won't do you any good unless you arrive
        safely,
    but arriving safely won't do you any good unless
        you arrive at the right place.
    Be blessed with the company of Thor, for safety.
    Be blessed with the company of Odin, the Knower
        of the Way,
    for arrival at the right place.

*Varuṇa:*

★   As I have sought forgiveness from,
    and given compensation to,
    those I have wronged,

I seek forgiveness of,
and burn this butter to,
you, Varuṇa:
may your snares, which enclose wrongdoers, pass
    me by.

★  If we have done that which is wrong,
breaking the laws of gods and of men,
may Varuṇa's snares still miss us.
Next time we will do better.

## Travel

★  This road is all roads:
my prayers to this road is to all roads on which I will
    travel.

★  On the open road
open me to all I encounter
Lord of All Ways.

★  Lord of the Pathways,
go before us on this trip,
and bring us safely and happily to our destination,
we who are your grateful followers.

★  This road I step on joins with all the other roads,
    forming an irregular net over the Earth, as if we
    could capture Her, an absurd and forlorn hope:

the net is only a decoration for her, like a golden
  hairnet on a beautiful woman.
So as I set myself on the road,
as I begin my traveling,
I make this offering to the Lord of Paths,
and I make offering to Earth.
But this net, and all roads, end at the sea.
So surprisingly, as I begin this travel across the land,
  I make offering to the Sea God, who receives all
  roads in the end, and thus encompasses all travelers on them.
Rider on the Waves, may the enclosing be of protection, not incarceration.
And even the sea is in the care of the Earth, lying
  across Her like a jewel around the neck of a
  beautiful woman,
and even the Sea God Her child.
So I make this fourth and final offering before setting
  out to the Earth,
ending my prayer where all roads and sea and traveling begins.

★  Both Healers and Guides,
   go with the ambulance I'm pulling over for.

*Air Spirits:*

★  The Spirits of the Air play about this plane as it flies.
   May they seek their fun in keeping its flight smooth
   rather than tossing it around.

May they compete among themselves to see which
    of them can best succeed in this.

*Castor and Pollux:*

★  Dioskouroi, Saviors,
    bring me through this storm:
    safely on the shore I will offer to you.

*Earth:*

★  From the air, I can best see the land below,
    the land below, spreading out,
    spreading out, Mother Earth,
    Mother Earth, your airborne child praises you.

★  Wide-Extending Earth,
    who cares for her children as a mother should:
    be smooth, be without obstruction,
    beneath and before me,
    as I travel on this journey.
    Bring me to my destination and home again safely,
    to contentment.

*The Elements:*

★  Air, be wind for his sails.
    Fire, be sun on his face.
    Water, be smooth ocean beneath him.
    Earth, be the island from which he sails.
    All this on a safe journey to his desired destination.

*Forest Spirits:*

★  Into the forest, laughing,
    guide my feet, Spirits of Nature;

into its depths, conduct my heart;
into its mysteries, initiate my soul.

*Gaṇeśa:*

★ Dancing Gaṇeśpati,
Trumpet the jet engines' roars of my plane,
clearing the way.

*The God and Goddess:*

★ Lord of grain and animals,
Lady of fruits and plants,
may I find a place to eat off this exit.

*Hekate:*

★ My prayer today is to Hekate:
may the fire with which I bless you be one of her
    torches,
going before you to guide you on your way.
May she whom even Zeus honors, and who receives
    a portion of every prayer,
hear this one;
may she provide a light, not just of protection until
    you reach your destination,
but to illuminate you that you might not miss the
    beauty of the journey in anticipation of your
    goal.

*Herakles:*

★ Wanderer,
Laborer,

who never rested until you laid yourself,
live and in pain,
on your own funeral pyre,
lit by a friend,
from which to rise, once mortal,
to a seat among the immortal gods:
Traveler, aid those who travel;
aid me on my way.
Succeeder in trials,
bring me to success through your invincible
    strength:
closest of the gods to man.

*Land Spirits:*

★ Spirits of the land we're driving through,
hand us off, each to the next,
smoothly as we go.
We honor each of you with this prayer.

*Lords of Space and Time:*

★ Time is Space, and Space is Time;
Space-Time is the fabric of the Cosmos.
I'm a little embarrassed to invoke such a thing for
    such a little reason, Lord of Space and Time, but
    it's like this:
I'm late for an appointment.
As the time grows less, may the space grow less
    rapidly.

I'm not asking you to bend the rules of physics,
just to make the way smooth for those ahead of me,
so that it might be smooth for me,
so that I'll arrive in time, or at least not too late.

*Manannán mac Lir:*

★ May my car flow through the undulating traffic as
    effortlessly as your chariot over the flower-
        plained ocean,
Manannán mac Lir,
you whose waves are horses.

★ Oirbsen mac Lir,
smoothly sailing, and safely to shore,
God of the journey, to you I pray:
go before me, clear the way.

★ Manannán, guide my flight today.
May my airplane's wings rise like sails,
likes wings of gulls.
May the air be smooth,
be like a flowered plain beneath your chariot wheels.

*Poseidon:*

★ A horse among horses be this boat,
under the protection of the god of horses,
god of the sea, of white-maned horses.

*River Spirits:*

★ Proud River, I give you this respectful thought as I
    cross this bridge over you.

Even if I myself don't endure struggles as I cross,
    [river name],
remember that those who built this bridge did,
and consider [these words/this offering] an addition
    to theirs.

*Sea:*

★ Happily arrived in harbor, I offer this thanksgiving
    coin to the sea.

*Woden:*

★ A companion makes the way shorter,
or sweeter,
and the load lighter.
Walk with me, Woden.
Even when I don't see you, I'll know you're there by
    the mysteries spoken in my heart,
from the wisdom-patterned sound of my feet
    against the ground,
echoed by yours.

★ A road-weary traveler, trudging beside me,
lifts hand to hat as if in salute;
his one eye winks, and laughter follows.
Woden, Lord of the Way,
do not lead me lost,
make my road right,
Old Rambler, you.

# CHAPTER 18

# SOCIETY AND THE LAND

We live not just by ourselves—as families, in homes. We are social creatures, and we gather together in groups that then have their own needs. Societies have to function smoothly, provide protection for their members, and continue to exist. As the preamble to the Constitution of the United States says, they exist to "establish justice, insure domestic tranquility, provide for the common defense, [and] promote the general welfare."

Living in society, we must govern ourselves. Although separation of church and state remains an ideal, we are free ourselves (and maybe even obligated) to seek the guidance of the divine in our own governmental relationships. We will keep an oath more faithfully if it is taken by our gods. We will vote more responsibly if we pray to the goddess Democracy. Our elected officials may perform their duties more effectively if the deities have greased the wheels of society.

## Society

★ Here in this city, surrounded by a canyon of
   buildings that seem to block out Nature,
   I pray to the gods of nature, who are present
   everywhere,

here no less than in the wild forest,
or the empty plains over which the storm winds blow,
or the ocean that hides its immense numbers of life
    in its depths.
For we human beings are not separate from Nature,
and have our own nature,
and this nature is above all to gather into
    communities,
and to form societies,
and to build cities.
So I stand here in this city and praise Nature,
present here all around us.
How could we keep Her out?

★ Open my eyes, Dyếus Ptếr, to those around me.
Open my heart, Gʷouwindā, with your loving care.
Unite me with them, Xáryomen,
into a society of individuals,
based on reciprocal exchange.

*Commerce:*

★ Commerce is not just a means, but an end. The
    buying and selling, the trade that Commerce
    is, unites people in strong bonds. Commerce is
    therefore one of the bases of community.
Thanks to Commerce, then, for establishing and
    contributing to our society. We serve you in
    this way:

by dealing fairly, but with an eye on profit, thereby
contributing to human society, ourselves acting
like you.
If imitation is the sincerest form of flattery, be flat-
tered by our commerce and join with us,
Commerce, god of prosperous social relationships.

*Individualism and Community:*

★ Individualism and Community are married,
inseparable,
neither ever found without the other.
Community without Individualism would be
despotism;
Independence with Community, wandering lost.
When I pray to you, then, I will always pray to the
both,
as two separate ones joined together.
This is how I pray to you today,
asking that you strengthen the individual society,
blessing us with both freedom and confraternity.

*Mitra:*

★ Grasp my hand, Mitra, as I hold it out to you.
I offer fairly to you, and you to me.
We are fair traders, you and I.
And I vow to you that all with whom I trade will be
to me as you.
I will be honest in my dealings with them,

give value for value,
as you do to me.

*Quirinus:*

★ Amid the flow of people on this street, I find
      Quirinus, God of Peoples,
God of *my* people,
and praise him with my steps,
their rhythm blending with those of the others
      among whom I live and move.

*Shang Ti:*

★ From your high mountain, dispense justice.
Impose, Shang Ti, peace-bringing order.

## Urban Prayers

★ Each building an obelisk erected in honor of the
      multitude of gods of my community,
the many gods of the many beliefs of the many
      people from who it is formed.

★ We plant seeds in the ground and water them, and
      plants grow,
each with their own spirit.
We quarry stone, smelt ore, and buildings grow,
each with their own spirit.
A forest of trees has a spirit.
A city of buildings has a spirit.

Through the forests roam the gods and spirits of the
    forest.
Through the cities roam the gods and spirits of the
    cities.
Entering the [forest/city] I say this prayer to the gods
    and spirits of this place
and to those of the [city/forest] I am leaving.

★  Every pattern is holy,
    even these roads I'm driving on.
    Every pattern has a spirit,
    even these roads I'm driving on.
    I forget that sometimes, though,
    so please forgive me,
    and I'll sometime give you an offering.

★  The Works of Man are the works of Nature,
    for Man is of the World.
    The towering buildings of this city stand as nobly as
        ancient trees,
    grown tall with age.
    My praise goes out to those who built them,
    whether living or dead,
    for their skill and vision,
    and to the Ancestors who developed the means to
        build them,
    and to the spirit of the city itself,
    formed of and forming the city around us.

*The All-Gods:*

★ In the midst of a busy city, the gods crowd close,
  each asking for worship,
  the gods of each and all.
  You are so many that I can't begin to honor you one
      by one:
  take these words as a gift to you all.

*Xáryomen:*

★ Lying awake in the dark of an unfamiliar city,
  I can feel the hum that extends through it and holds
      it together.
  I feel the power lines, the water mains, the roads.
  I feel the bus routes, the subway tunnels, the
      bridges.
  I feel the police, the fire fighters, the EMTs,
  the garbage men, the delivery trucks,
  the hospitals, schools, and post offices.
  I feel the network that forms the city,
  its skeleton and capillaries,
  supporting and feeding it.
  And I feel your skeleton and capillaries,
  supporting and feeding it.
  And I know who you are
  and find myself familiar in an unfamiliar city.

## Government

★  We aren't governed by kings anymore,
    but those who do govern us still need the Truth of
        the King.
    So all the gods of kingship—Jupiter, Lugh, Indra,
        Osiris, Mitra,
    don't desert us.
    In this changed time, we still look to you for help.

★  President, Chief Executive, Commander-in-Chief:
    you have sworn to preserve, protect, and defend the
        Constitution.
    Gods and Goddesses of the Oath:
    don't let him forget this.
    And if he does, torment his dreams,
    compelling him to return to his vow.

★  Industry, you have made us strong.
    Commerce, you have made us rich.
    Agriculture, you have fed us well.
    War, you have defended our freedom.
    Peace, you have given us something to defend.
    Justice, you have enabled us to deserve all these.
    Liberty: with these we have built a home for you,
    and we ask you to come live with us,
    continually reminding us of your gifts and your
        demands.

★  We call you, Justice, to come,
   no matter what the cost to ourselves.
   We call you, Liberty, to come,
   no matter what sacrifices you may demand.
   We call you, Wisdom, to come,
   no matter how wrong we may prove to be.
   Bless America with your presence.
   Challenge America with your demands.
   Make all our actions prosperous and true.

★  Open the doors, Janus.
   Break down the walls, Thor.
   Burn through the chains, Agni.
   Show the way out, Amaterasu.
   All the gods, bring freedom to those in your lands,
   bring freedom to those in other lands,
   bring freedom to all in all lands.
   For by right of birth we are free,
   and meant to live by Liberty's decree.

*Ancestors:*

★  It might be that your blood doesn't flow through
        my veins,
   but your ideas flow through my mind.
   Founders and Framers,
   each day may I think of them,
   and each day work to bring them into being.

★ On an incomprehensibly vast ocean
To an unknowably deep land;
Trusting to wood and rope and cloth,
and fickle winds,
you came from a need to live as you thought right.
Though I do not like all you did,
and though you would not like all *I* do,
still like calls to like.
The fire in my heart is yours.
Against obstacles, you prevailed,
afraid below decks while storms shook the boat, you
      carried on.
If I, like you, set my self only to the right,
without the storms destroying my resolve,
I will consider myself truly your descendant.
As like calls to like, as fire to fire,
be with me and give me courage as needed.

*Democracy:*

★ It's not your hands I'm voting with, Demokratia,
so don't let anyone try to tell you that.
I mean, really, what would be the point?
If my vote isn't independently given it's not under
      your blessing.
It's only when I don't ask you how to vote that I can
      really honor you.
Freedom is your worship.

*Genius of the People:*

★ In times past, people prayed to the deities who ruled governments to bless their society, to ensure good government. They prayed to the god who guided the rule, or the genius of the ruler, or to the ruler himself.

We don't do that. We have no ruler toward whom we might pray, or to whose genius we might pray, or to whose guiding deity we might pray. Or we *do* have a ruler, but not one; we have many. For our ruler is the People. So if we are to pray for our ruler we must pray to the genius of the polity itself, not to give power, but authority; not to ease the application of force, but its right use; to gain liberty and justice for each person, and for the People.

Make us a moral nation, Genius; that is, one in which each citizen is continually trying to both know and practice Virtue. Instill in us and encourage in us a love for the Good. This is the only way to pray for our ruler; be pleased by our knowing that.

*Liberty:*

★ Liberty
Mother of Exiles
Hear your children as we call to you!

You have watched over our nation,
keeping it free,
keeping it independent,
for [number of years] years you have done this,
faithfully and carefully,
with love for your children.
Liberty
Mother of Exiles
Hear your children as we call to you!
Be with us now as you have been with us from our
    beginning.

★ Many and great are the gifts Liberty brings.
Many and great are the forms in which she comes
    to us.
We praise her in all of them.
Liberty of the Harbor,
may your flame shine to light the whole world.
Armed Freedom,
may you watch over our government.
Walking Liberty,
may it be the rising sun of prosperity from which
    you stride.
Libertas!
Liberté!
Liberty!
We remember you in all of your forms

and worship you in all of the ways you show yourself
    to us.

★ Here today, I would like to invoke the sacred name
    of Liberty.

It was for Liberty that our ancestors fought.

It was with her inspiration that they created our
    Constitution.

It was with her guidance that they formed a nation.

It was for her continuing inspiration that I pray
    today.

The Founders had a vision:

a land fit for Liberty to dwell in.

Under her guidance we will make that dream real.


★ Liberty:

Our Representatives and Senators,

Our President,

Our Supreme Court,

only hold their offices to make you known.

Make this known to *them*,

so that knowing you they will be inspired to your
    service.


★ Whether with bound-back or loose hair,

the cap of your pole bites deeper than an iron spear
    tip on any others.

Whether through images or ideas, words or deeds,

may you triumph throughout the world!
Praised in the past by few,
Praised today by many,
May you, Liberty, be praised in the future by all
    throughout the world,
by all nations and cultures,
your torch a light to all!

*Liberty and Minerva:*

★  Renew your old friendship, Minerva and Liberty,
create a land where creativity runs free and freedom
    possesses the skills to become real.
Work without freedom is enslaving;
Freedom without work, pointless.
Work without freedom is deadening;
Freedom without work, lifeless.
Renew your ancient friendship, Minerva and Liberty,
and inspire the citizens of this country to create a
    land where you'll feel at home.

★  Sweet Liberty,
whose self-evident truths can be so hard to see,
and so hard to establish,
and so hard to maintain:
to you, increased devotion.
Minerva, through whose wisdom the founding
    documents were composed,
and through whose martial power liberty has been
    maintained,

and through whose teachings of skill the People
    have prospered:
increased devotion.
To America, ever young and learning,
ever unfolding the lessons of Liberty taught by
    Minerva:
listen to them well.
With you,
as part of you,
I worship Liberty and Minerva today,
and will each day,
with increased devotion.

*Mars:*

★ With your weapons and armor, Father Mars,
protect our land.
With your weapons and armor, Father Mars,
protect our Constitution.
The one to prevent our destruction
The other to make us worthy of emulation.

*Providence:*

★ The founding deities,
Liberty, Justice, Democracy, and the others,
are continually unfolded by us into a country more
    and more in accord with their teachings.
Liberty denied to blacks was extended to them with
    the abolition of slavery.

Justice denied to the indigent was extended to them
     by requiring public defenders for those who
     could not pay.
Democracy denied to women was extended to
     them by the ratification of the Nineteenth
     Amendment,
so that our imperfect system grows closer and closer
     to the deities' perfection,
even if it does not operate perfectly itself, and
     sometimes denies even that which has been
     extended.
These changes are created by human beings,
but they do this as they apprehend more and more
     the implications of the self-evident truths on
     which America was founded.
This apprehension is itself the result of human effort,
but its inevitability and development in time,
so that each new perception of truth might be
     absorbed in preparation for the next,
are in the care of Providence, the deity which keeps
     us under its special protection,
and provides the means through which the other
     deities might perform their work.
This deity is hard to know, since it is itself one of
     knowing,
and how can one know the knower?

Indeed, whether Providence is a god or a goddess is
　　not even known.
So, having no shape, it is what *gives* shape,
Providence is shown in the Great Seal as the Eye and
　　the Pyramid:
the Eye which watches us,
and the unfinished Pyramid of the American ideals.
It is to Providence that we pray today,
that our sight might be clear, to see the founding
　　principles better,
and that we might find the strength to climb the
　　Pyramid again and again,
carrying more blocks of stones, to place them there,
　　strongly cementing them with mortar.
Providence asks us not for offerings of things, but of
　　words that inspire,
ideals in our minds,
and the continuing effort to defend and protect the
　　founding ideas.
Our vow today, then, is not to erect a stone altar, but
　　one that is informed of all that is good and right,
and conducive to the extension of the Self-Evident
　　Truths to all,
and not just to those who pray here.
And for that we ask strength and knowledge and
　　wisdom,

and most of all courage:
May we both know the right and do it.

*Rule of Law:*

★ Rule of Law, with your rods and axe,
gather us together,
enable the State to enforce the right only under your
    blessing and approval.

*Shang Ti:*

★ Shang Ti, ruler of all under heaven, rule benevolently
through the Eastern Mother,
through the Western Mother,
through the Ruler of the four quarters.
We offer to the East.
We offer to the West.
We offer to the North.
We offer to the South.
We offer in the way of the Way.
We offer with a request for your just governance of all.

## Justice

*Apollo:*

★ Son of Leto:
You whose chariot is the all-seeing sun,
whose truth-knowledge sees into every dark corner,
whose arrows strike down liars with no mistakes:
today in this court may only truth be spoken

may only truth be heard
may only truth be decided.
Phoebus Apollo, here my prayer.

*Hekate:*

★ Come to me,
but don't *go* to me, Hekate.
Go instead to those who unjustly oppose me
and torment them.
Be relentless.
My cause is right.
If not, may it be I who feels your wrath.

*Helios:*

★ It is true that you see everything that happens under
    you, Helios,
great eye of the heavens.
So you know that I am blameless in this matter
and you know who is to blame.
Harry them with guilt.
Beat down on them relentlessly and mercilessly
until they right the wrong.

*Justice:*

★ Not content with your blindfold's shield
you avert your eyes from the scales by which you
    separate the false from the true,
and even with your unseeing eyes the sword you
    carry will not miss,

separating the just from the unjust.
May all my deeds,
on this and other days,
be weighed as true
that I might be able to meet your piercing nongaze
    without fear.

*Maat:*

★ If what I'm doing is right,
    a touch as light as the feather of Maat will suffice.
    Goddess of Truth,
    turn my feet onto the path of the Good.

*Tyr:*

★ Irony of ironies, that you, God of the Oath,
    have no right hand to raise in swearing.
    Or perhaps just right, needing nothing to show for
        your speaking,
    the speaking alone being enough.
    Even thus, though I raise my hand as a sign of truth
        to others,
    to you and to me the words suffice,
    writing my vow into the Ørlog.

## Peace

★ In time of war, we come together as a people,
    as a people, we must pray for peace:
    Holy Ones, may there be peace.

In time of war, we come together in our families,
as families, we must pray for peace:
Holy Ones, may there be peace.
In time of war, we find ourselves as individuals,
as individuals, we must pray for peace:
Holy Ones, may there be peace.
As a people, as families, as individuals, we must pray
     for peace:
Holy Ones, bring us peace.

*The Goddess, for peace:*

★  Peace, sweet Peace,
   bring to this divided land,
   Comforting Mother of the soothing hand.

*Peace:*

★  On wings that light away war's shadows, fly swiftly
        to us, Peace,
   to those who wait impatiently after praying.
   We pray for Peace,
   we pray to Peace.
   To Peace, Goddess of Promise,
   Holy and Pure One, we pray for peace.

## The Land

★  Spirits of plants and animals,
   of water and stone;
   All the Spirits of this land:

Our ancestors weren't kind to your ancestors when
  they came to this land.
Today, hear our words,
taste our offerings,
so we might begin a new relationship with you,
a few small steps on the road to trust.
May they bless us, these beings of numinous
  presence,
when we bring them our gifts of offerings and words
with minds well-intentioned, with hearts
  well-inclined,
in worship, in honor, with well-deserved reverence.
May those worthy of blessing bless all who pray:
Holy Ones, this prayer from me to you.

# APPENDIX A

## Index of Offerings

Gods have personal tastes just as we do, and offerings to them will vary from deity to deity. If you're expecting a dinner guest you know doesn't like peas, how rude is it to serve peas? You're not likely to develop a relationship that way. Or worse; who would knowingly serve pork to an observant Jew? That would not only be offensive; it would be an offense. The same is true with deities. Some are offended by certain offerings—most commonly, meat, which is particularly bothersome to some domestic deities.

Sometimes, you can find out what to offer deities through research. Cultures often have traditions: water mixed with wine for Greek deities, sake for Japanese kami, etc. Individual deities may also have preferences. For instance, we know from Apuleius (*Golden Ass*, 3.27) that Epona liked roses. But sometimes, you will need to experiment, starting with what seems best and seeing what happens.

There are some patterns linking deity type and offerings that can help with this. The following list gives some of them. These suggestions are not meant to be taken as hard and fast rules—a deity from a culture that does not drink milk may be confused by a milk offering—but they can give you a starting point for experimentation.

In the following list, animals can be replaced with meat or symbolic offerings.

**ANCESTORS:** Food and drink from the family table, bread (especially dark), beer, beans, caraway, hair. If you are offering to a particular ancestor, use their favorite foods.

**BIRTH DEITIES:** Bread, eggs, milk, sandalwood, mint, roses.

**BORDER GUARDIANS:** Pigs, eggs, honey, milk, wine, flower garlands.

**CULTURE DEITIES:** Songs, poems, prepared food.

**DEATH DEITIES:** Pork, dogs, beer. This is one exception to the rule of sharing; you don't want to share with death.

**DEITIES IN GENERAL:** Bread, butter or oil (burned), wine, beer, frankincense.

**EARTH DEITIES:** Bread, pigs, beer.

**FIRE DEITIES:** Flammable items, especially liquids like vegetable oils, whiskey, or melted clarified butter.

**GARDEN SPIRITS:** Bread, grain, fruit, water, milk, honey, bay leaf incense, flowers.

**HEARTH GUARDIANS:** Bread, butter, milk, pine incense, rosemary. Generally not meat.

**HOUSE SPIRITS:** Bread, salt, wine, milk, food from the family table, butter, beer.

**LUNAR DEITIES:** Milk, bread, white flowers.

**NATURE SPIRITS IN GENERAL:** Local grain (cornmeal in America, wheat or barley in England, etc.), bread, beer, flowers, shiny things.

**NATURE SPIRITS (AMERICAN):** Cornmeal, sage, tobacco, shiny things.

**SOLAR DEITIES:** Horses, white wine, mead, gold, butter.

**STORM DEITIES:** Cattle, beer, meteorites, sledge hammers, axes, flint.

**TECHNOLOGY DEITIES:** Tools, products of labor.

**THRESHOLD GUARDIANS:** Barley, bread, wine, juniper.

**WAR DEITIES:** Cattle, goats, iron, weapons.

# APPENDIX B

## Glossary of Deities

**Aengus Óg:** Irish. God of youth, love, and inspiration.

**Agni:** "Fire." Vedic. God of fire, priest of the gods, intermediary between us and the gods.

**Airmed:** Irish. Goddess of healing, especially with herbs.

**Airyamen:** "The People." Vedic. God of society, healing, and marriage; of bringing things together happily.

**Amaterasu:** Japanese. Sun goddess.

**Apam Napat:** "Close Relative of the Waters." God of fire hidden in water; often identified with Agni.

**Aphrodite:** Greek. The Greeks translated her name as "foam born," but it probably has its origin in "Ashtorerth," the name of the Phoenecian version of Astarte. Goddess of love, beauty, and passion.

**Apollo:** Greek and Roman. God of healing, truth, civilization, music, and the sun.

**Ares:** "Strife." Greek. God of war.

**Ariomanus:** Roman. A god in Mithraism depicted with a lion's head and wings. He likely was a god of fire who served to purify the soul on its journey toward the celestial realm.

**Artemis:** Greek. Goddess of the wild, the hunt, virginity, and the moon.

**Asklepios:** Greek (in Rome, he was called "Aesculapius"). God of healing.

**Athena:** "Of Athens." Greek. Goddess of wisdom, communication, and the practical arts; also of politics and protection. Equivalent to the Roman Minerva.

**Aushrine:** "Rising." Lithuanian. Goddess of the dawn and spring.

**BRIGHID:** "Exalted." Irish. Hearth goddess, mothering goddess. As patron of poets, smiths, and healers, she is also a goddess of inspiration.

**CASTOR AND POLLUX:** Greek and Roman. Twin gods, protectors, especially of sailors and soldiers. Patrons of cattle and horse ranchers.

**CERES:** "Grower." Roman. Goddess of growing things, especially grain, and of prosperity.

**CERNUNNOS:** "Antlered One." Gaulish. The one who goes between opposites; god of prosperity, especially that acquired through trade.

**CYBELE:** Phrygian. Mother goddess.

**DIONYSOS:** Greek. God of wine, the vine, and ecstasy.

**DOMOVOI:** Russian. House guardian who lives behind the stove.

**DYÉUS PTÉR:** "Shining Sky Father." Proto-Indo-European. Chief god, dispenser of wisdom and justice, enforcer of the natural order of things.

**EOS:** "Rising." Greek. Goddess of the spring and dawn.

**EOSTRE:** "Rising." Germanic. Goddess of the spring and dawn.

**FIREBIRD:** Russian. A bird that dwells in a faraway land, guarding the Tree of Life. It may bring blessings or disaster on those who encounter it.

**FREYR:** "Lord." Norse. God of friendship, fertility, and sexuality.

**GAṆEŚA:** "Lord of Categories." Hindu. An elephant-headed god, overcomer of obstacles.

**GENIUS:** "One Who Gives Birth." Roman. A divine being who is intimately connected with a certain thing—a person, an area, a group of people, etc.

**THE GOD:** Wiccan. The male principle personified, with attributes such as death, power, and sexuality.

**THE GODDESS:** Wiccan. The female principle personified, with attributes such as birth, fertility, and sexuality.

**Green Man:** Modern Pagan. A personification of the forces of the wild, especially of forests.

**Gʷouwindā:** "Giver of Cows." Proto-Indo-European. A goddess of prosperity.

**Hathor:** "House of Horus." Egyptian. A very complicated goddess, mixing motherhood, sexuality, fertility, death, and protection. She was often depicted with a cow's head.

**Hearth goddess:** Found in many cultures, she is seen as being present on the hearth as the fire itself. The most famous hearth goddesses are the Irish Brighid, Roman Vesta, and Greek Hestia.

**Hekate:** Greek. Goddess of witchcraft, the crossroads, and justice.

**Helios:** "Sun." Greek. God of the sun, as the great "eye in the sky," he sees the deeds of men, and is thus a god of justice, truth, and sight.

**Hephaestus:** Greek. God of smiths and potters, and thus of artisans in general.

**Herakles:** "Glory of Hera." Greek (in Rome, he was called "Hercules"). Hero god; originally half-human, he knows what it's like to be one of us. Because he had to wander so far in his Twelve Labors, he protects travelers, and also merchants.

**Hermes:** Greek. Messenger of the gods, leader of the soul to the land of the dead. Also a god of magic, commerce, travel, thieves, and skills.

**Herne:** "Horn." English. A hunting god; the name is often used by Wiccans as one of the names of their God.

**Horus:** "Distant (or "Superior") One." Egyptian. God of the sun, hero god, destroyer of evil.

**Inanna:** "Lady of the Sky." Sumerian. Goddess of sexuality, life, death, and kingship.

**Indra:** "Man, Hero." Vedic. Protector, warrior, god of the thunderstorm.

**Iris:** Greek. Goddess of the rainbow and, in early times, the messenger of the gods.

**Isis:** "Throne." Egyptian. Mother goddess, sovereignty goddess.

**Janus:** "Doorway." Roman. God of beginnings and of doors; he was shown with two faces—one looking one way, one looking the other—showing that he was the god of the moment between one thing and another.

**Jupiter:** "Shining Sky Father." Roman. Head of the gods, and a god of justice.

**Kami:** Japanese. The term for any spiritual being; it can be used for either the singular or the plural.

**Kindreds:** The sacred figures seen as a whole, encompassing the deities, the Ancestors, the land spirits, etc.

**Kwan Yin:** Buddhist. A divine being of mercy and compassion. Also spelled *Guan Yin*.

**Lleu Llaw Gyffes:** "Bright One with the Steady Hand." Welsh. Champion god, god of kingship and justice.

**Lugh:** "Shining," or perhaps "Champion." Irish. God of lightning, kingship, protection, and agriculture. He is called "He of many skills," and is a patron of artisans.

**Maat:** "Truth, Order." Egyptian. Goddess of justice, not in the legal sense, but in that of doing the right thing. It is by her that the rightness of our actions is determined.

**Manannán mac Lir:** Irish. A god of the sea and of wisdom. *Mac Lir* means "Son of the Sea," which is probably not meant to indicate who his father was, but what he was associated with. His earliest name was probably Oirbsen.

**Marduk:** Possibly "Bull Calf of the Sun." Babylonian. A god of lordship, protection, and war, he fought against Chaos and created the Cosmos from her body.

**MARS:** Roman. God of war and agriculture; likely originally one of thunder.

**THE MARUTS:** Vedic. A warrior troop that accompanies Indra and may originally have been connected with thunder.

**MENOT:** "Moon, Measurer." Proto-Indo-European. God of the moon, and, because the moon measures out time, of measurement and right thinking.

**MERCURY:** Roman. A go-between—messenger of the gods, protector of merchants (and thus a god of wealth), guide to the land of the dead. Also a god of knowledge.

**MINERVA:** Posssibly "Thought." Roman. Goddess of wisdom, communication, and the practical arts; also of politics and protection. Equivalent to the Greek Athena.

**MITHRA:** "Contract." Vedic. God of the human laws, protector from the vagaries of the divine. In later Sanskrit, his name becomes the everyday word for "friend."

**MITHRAS:** Roman. The god at the center of a mystery cult that seems to have been based on the idea of the development of the soul into a level of divinity. Not the same god as either Mithra or Mitra.

**MITRA:** "Contract." Iranian. Enforcer of agreements, god of justice, protector of friendship.

**MORPHEUS:** "Shaper, Molder." Greek. God of sleep.

**MORRÍGAIN:** "Nightmare Queen." Irish. Goddess of sovereignty, war, and sexuality.

**NUIT:** Thelemic. Goddess of the stars, of infinite possibility, and of the great Void.

**ODIN:** "Ecstatic One." Norse. God of war, wisdom, magic, and inspiration.

**OGHMA:** "Writing." Irish. God of writing and thought.

**OSIRIS:** Egyptian. God of the land of the dead.

PAN: "Nourisher, Protector." Greek. God of the pastures, that is, of the land between the domesticated and the wild. Bringer of divine madness.

PELE: Hawaiian. Goddess of the volcano.

PERKʷÚNOS: "Striker" or "Oak God." Proto-Indo-European. Protector, warrior, god of the thunderstorm. Patron of farmers.

PERSEPHONE: Greek. Goddess of the spring and of new growth, but also the queen of the dead.

POSEIDON: Possibly "Lord of Earth." Greek. God of the ocean, earthquakes, and horses.

PŪṢAN: "Protector" or "Nourisher." Vedic. God of merchants and travel; conveyor of brides.

QUIRINUS: "God of the Assembly." Roman. God of the people as a whole.

RHIANNON: "Great Queen." Welsh. Goddess of sovereignty and of wisdom.

SARASVATI: "Marshy." Hindu. Goddess of speech, eloquence, poetry, the arts, and music.

SELENE: "Moon." Greek. Goddess of the moon.

SEQUANA: Gaulish. Goddess of the river Seine.

SHANG TI: "Celestial Lord." Chinese. The creator god, the divine version of the Emperor. Also spelled "Shangdi."

SILVANUS: "Lord of the Forest." Roman. Originally a god of the forest, he came to be seen as also the protector of the land that had been carved out of the forest, and thus of property and those who inhabit it.

SOMA: "The Pressed Out." Vedic. Personification of a drink that brought ecstasy; in later Hinduism, god of the moon.

TAHUTI: Egyptian. God of writing, magic, and wisdom.

TARANIS: "Thunder." Gaulish. God of the thunderstorm.

TERMINUS: "Border." Roman. God of borders and border stones.

THOR: "Thunder." Norse. Protector, warrior, god of the thunderstorm. Patron of farmers.

THOTH: Egyptian; god of writing, magic, and wisdom. The Greek spelling of "Tahuti."

THUNDERBIRD: American Indian. Spirit/god of the storm, especially of the beginning of the rainy season in desert areas.

TYR: "Shining." Norse. God of the oath and of war.

UṢAS "Rising." Goddess of the dawn, the sister of night. Often spelled "Ushas."

VĀC: "Word." Vedic. Goddess of speech.

VARUṆA "Encloser." Vedic. Enforcer of the moral order, both social and cosmic.

VAYŪ: "Wind." Vedic. God of the wind.

VENUS: "Desire." Roman. Goddess of love and beauty.

VIṢṆU: Hindu. Creation of the extent of the world, and its sustainer. Often spelled "Vishnu."

VULCAN: Roman. God of smiths and potters, and thus of artisans.

WESTYĀ: "She of the Household." Proto-Indo-European. A hearth goddess.

WODEN: "Ecstatic One." Anglo-Saxon. God of wisdom, magic, inspiration, and travel.

XÁKWŌM NÉPŌT: "Relative of the Waters." Proto-Indo-European. Protector of a well of fiery water that inspires and enlivens, but that is dangerous to those who aren't worthy to drink from it.

XÁRYOMEN: "God of our People." Proto-Indo-European. God of society, healing, and marriage; of bringing things together happily.

ZEUS: "Shining." Greek. Chief of the gods; lord of justice, lightning, and hospitality.

*On all who have worshipped here,*
*Inspiration, power, peace.*
*On all who revere the Holy Ones,*
*Inspiration, power, peace.*
*On who walk the ancient path,*
*Inspiration, power, peace.*

# WORKS CITED

## GENERAL REFERENCES

Hayakawa, S. I. *Choose the Right Word: A Modern Guide to Synonyms*. New York: Harper and Row, 1968.

Nelson, John K. *A Year in the Life of a Shinto Shrine*. Seattle: University of Washington Press, 1996.

Nicolson, Adam. *God's Secretaries: The Making of the King James Bible*. New York: HarperCollins, 2003.

Redford, Donald B. (ed.). *The Oxford Essential Guide to Egyptian Mythology*. New York: Oxford University Press, 2003.

Staal, Frits. *Agni: The Vedic Ritual of the Fire Altar* (2 vol.). Delhi: Motilal Banarsidass, 1983.

Tolkien, J. R. R. *The Lays of Beleriand*. Boston: Houghton Mifflin, 1985.

———. *The Legend of Sigurd and Gudrún*. Ed. Christopher Tolkien. A modern version of a medieval Germanic tale, told in the alliterative style. Good discussion of Germanic poetic style.

Watkins, Calvert. *How to Kill a Dragon: Aspects of Indo-European Poetics*. New York: Oxford University Press, 1995. An analysis of Indo-European poetry, especially meters. Most of the texts are prayers from ancient cultures. Very technical.

West, M. L. *Indo-European Poetry and Myth*. New York: Oxford University Press, 2007. Deals with the form and imagery of Indo-European poetry, as well as basic religion. Many excerpts from prayers and hymns. Not as technical as Watkins.

Willis, Garry. *Lincoln at Gettysburg: The Words that Remade America*. New York: Simon and Schuster, 1992.

## PRAYERS AND RITUAL

Adkins, Lesley and Roy A. Adkins. *Dictionary of Roman Religion*. New York: Oxford University Press, 1996. Descriptions of Roman deities, and many Gaulish ones.

*www.avesta.org/avesta.html*. Includes translations of all the Zoroastrian hymns.

Bell, Catherine. *Ritual: Perspectives and Dimension*. New York: New York University Press, 1977. Academic, but not too hard a read.

*Book of Common Prayer.* www.eskimo.com/~lhowell/bcp1662/. Although Christian, the style of this book of devotions has shaped much of what we have come to expect from prayers. The imagery is wonderful, and the prayers are good examples of how noble spoken English can be.

Boyce, Mary (ed. and tr.). *Textual Sources for the Study of Zoroastrianism.* Manchester, UK: Manchester University Press, 1984. Includes translations of a number of Zoroastrian hymns, different from *http://avesta.org*, and perhaps more reliable.

Budge, E. A. Wallis. *The Gods of the Egyptians* (2 vols.). New York: Dover Publications, 1904. His translations are out-of-date, as are his commentaries, but they are all suggestive of the style of Egyptian prayers. Particularly valuable is that he gives many titles by which each deity may be called.

Carmichael, Alexander. *Carmina Gadelica: Hymns and Incantations Collected in the Highlands and Islands of Scotland in the Last Century.* Edinburgh: Lindisfarne Press, 1992 (1909). Originally published in four volumes in the late 19th/early 20th centuries. The original version included the Scots Gaelic; this edition does not. Christian, but with a Pagan appreciation for nature. Many Pagans have used prayers from this source, with the substitution of Pagan deities for the Christian God and saints.

Dangler, Michael J. (ed.). *The Fire on Our Hearth: A Devotional of Three Cranes Grove, ADF.* Columbus, OH: Three Cranes Grove, 2008. Rituals of a modern Druidic grove. Available from *www.threecranes.org*.

Eliade, Mircea. *Essential Sacred Writings from Around the World.* San Francisco: HarperSanFrancisco, 1967.

———. *The Sacred and the Profane.* New York: Harcourt Brace Jovanovich. The classic work on sacred space.

Evelyn-White, Hugh G. (tr.). *Hesiod, Homeric Hymns, Epic Cycle, Homerica.* Cambridge, MA: Harvard University Press, 1936. The Homeric Hymns are prayers to the Greek gods.

Fitch, Ed and Janet Renee. *Magical Rites from the Crystal Well.* St. Paul, MN: Llewellyn, 1984. Neo-Pagan rituals, with some beautiful prayers.

Hollander, Lee M. (tr.). *The Poetic Edda.* Austin, TX: University of Texas Press, 1962. Translation in a very Germanic poetic form of one of the major sources of Norse mythology.

Laurie, Erynn. *A Circle of Stones: Journeys and Meditations for Modern Celts.* Chicago: Eschaton, 1995. A rosary using Irish texts. Available for purchase as a PDF file at *www.seanet.com/~inisglas/publications.html*.

Lipp, Deborah. *The Elements of Ritual*. St. Paul, MN: Llewellyn, 2003. Wonderful book on ritual theory and practice. Much useful advice on the practical side of things.

Matasović, Ranko. *A Theory of Textual Reconstruction in Indo-European Linguistics*. New York: Peter Lang, 1996. Indo-European (primarily Vedic and Greek) poetic metaphors and structures.

McMahon, Gregory. *The Hittite State Cult of the Tutelary Deities (Assyriological Studies 25)*. Chicago: University of Chicago Press, 1991. Hittite rituals and prayers.

Panikkar, Raimundo. *The Vedic Experience*: *Mantramañjari*. Berkeley: University of California Press, 1977. Collection of excerpts from Vedic prayers and other texts. Available online at *www.himalayanacademy. com/resources/books/vedic_experience/VEIndex. html*.

Propp, V. J. *Down Along the River Volga: An Anthology of Russian Folk Lyrics*. Tr. and ed., Roberta Reeder. Philadelphia: University of Pennsylvania Press, 1975.

Rananujan, A. K. (tr.). *Speaking of Śiva*. New York: Penguin Books, 1973. Hymns to the Hindu god Śiva.

Regardie, Israel (ed.). *Gems from the Equinox*. Newburyport, MA: Red Wheel/ Weiser, 2007. Ceremonial magical rituals, with some lovely prayers.

*Rig Veda*. The *Rig Veda* is a collection of hymns from ancient India. There is no completely reliable English translation. However, except for those interested in academic research into Vedic religion, what's available will be enough. See Griffith, Ralph T. H. New York: Book of the Month Club, 1992. Completed in 1896, this version is dated (he translates all of one hymn and part of another that he considers indelicate not into English, but Latin), but complete. It's easy to find, and is even available online at *www.sacred-texts.com/hin/rigveda/*. See also Macdonell, Arthur Anthony. *A Vedic Reader for Students*. Designed, as the title implies, for those learning to read Sanskrit. It includes translations of thirty hymns and descriptions of the deities they're addressed to. Another good source is O'Flaherty, Wendy Doniger. New York: Penguin Classics, 1981. Incomplete (about one tenth of the hymns), and criticized by some scholars, but beautifully written and inspiring.

Roberts, Elizabeth and Elias Amidon (eds.). *Earth Prayers from Around the World: 365 Prayers, Poems, and Invocations Honoring the Earth*. San Francisco: HarperSanFrancisco, 1991. Prayers from around the world, in a number of religious traditions.

Serith, Ceisiwr. *A Book of Pagan Prayer*. Boston: Weiser Books, 2002. The first third presents the theory of how prayers are constructed and performed; the rest is a collection of prayers.

———. *Deep Ancestors: Practicing the Religion of the Proto-Indo-Europeans*. Tucson, AZ: ADF Publishing, 2009.

Lady Sheba. *The Book of Shadows*. St. Paul, MN: Llewellyn, 2002.

Sturluson, Snorri. *Edda*. Tr. Anthony Faulkes. Rutland, VT: Charles E. Tuttle Co., 1987. Snorri gives titles ("kennings") of deities, as well as Norse myths.

Wolkstein, Diane and Samuel Noah Kramer. *Inanna, Queen of Heaven and Earth: Her Stories and Hymns from Sumer*. New York: Harper and Row, 1983.

# POETRY

Frost, Robert. *The Poetry of Robert Frost: The Collected Poems, Complete and Unabridged*. Ed. Edward Connery Lathem. New York: Holt, Rinehart and Winston, 1979. A master of American poetic style, Frost uses nature imagery as metaphors for human life, linking us to the natural world. He was a close observer of seasons.

*Haiku*. There are many books on haiku and related verse forms, as well as many websites.

Heaney, Seamus (tr.). *Beowulf: A New Verse Translation*. New York: W. W. Norton, 2000. A translation of this classic that keeps to the Old English alliterative scheme, but loosely enough to correspond to modern English poetic sensibilities.

Shakespeare, William. Naturally. He demonstrates the thin line between prose and poetry.

Sturluson, Snorri. *Edda*. Norse poetic theory, including kennings.

Whitman, Walt. *The Complete Poems*. One of the prime inventors of American poetic style. The tendency of his poems to dissolve into lists is actually a good model for prayers.

Yeats, W. B. *The Poems: The Collected Works of W. B. Yeats*. Ed. Richard J. Finneran. New York: Simon and Schuster, 1997. The most famous poet of the Celtic Revival, Yeats nevertheless wrote in English. This gives us a feel for how Irish rhythms and imagery can be adopted by English writers.